W9-DEO-730

CELLO TECHNIQUE

Gerhard Mantel

CELLO TECHNIQUE

Principles and Forms of Movement

TRANSLATED BY

BARBARA HAIMBERGER THIEM

INDIANA UNIVERSITY PRESS

Bloomington & London

Authorized English version based on the German original,
Cellotechnik: Bewegungsprinzipien und Bewegungsformen
by Gerhard Mantel, copyright © 1972 by Musikverlage Hans Gerig,
Köln/Cologne, West Germany. English translation copyright © 1975
by Indiana University Press.

All rights reserved

No part of this book may be reproduced or utilized in any form
or by any means, electronic or mechanical, including photocopying
and recording, or by any information storage and retrieval system,
without permission in writing from the publisher. The Association
of American University Presses Resolution on Permissions constitutes
the only exception to this prohibition.

Published in Canada by Fitzhenry & Whiteside Limited,
Don Mills, Ontario

Manufactured in the United States of America

Library of Congress Cataloging in Publication Data

Mantel, Gerhard.
Cello technique.

Bibliography.
1. Violoncello--Instruction and study. I. Title.
MT300.M313   787'.3'0712   75-7233
ISBN 0-253-31327-9   1 2 3 4 5 79 78 77 76 75

CONTENTS

ALMA COLLEGE
MONTEITH LIBRARY
ALMA, MICHIGAN

FOREWORD

Whenever a political candidate is asked to express his opinion on any given issue the safest cliché is "not enough is being done about . . . ," and any subject can be named to fill in the dots. His opponent says the same, and both are safe and right.

All through my professional life, when receiving or finding works pertaining to cello playing, I could not help but express the above cliché. "It is not enough!" Books with many valid points invariably fell short of answering or dealing with unlimited numbers of issues. Methods are usually directed toward special problems and aimed at particular groups of players.

The major value of Gerhard Mantel's book is that no one can say that it is "not enough." It discusses all conceivable aspects of cello playing in the utmost clinical detail. It is based on honest research, experiment, and experience. As such it can help to eliminate much harmful teaching of baseless principles, usually the result of individual teachers' playing shortcomings. It can promote the recognition of many proven facts, though often contradictory to accepted traditions. It can even help to explain various schools of playing where the differences may be real, semantic, or matters of taste.

In such an undertaking there is an inherent danger that statements may sound dogmatic, although arguments, discussions, and disagreements are called for. Nevertheless, I urge that this book be obligatory reading for those whose aim in life is the responsibility of teaching future generations to play the cello.

JANOS STARKER

BLOOMINGTON, INDIANA

JUNE 1974

TRANSLATOR'S NOTE

Gerhard Mantel's *Cello Technique* accomplishes what few other books on the subject do: it gives both teacher and student a vocabulary with which to conceptualize and discuss what happens when the cello is played. For this reason I decided to take time off from a busy schedule as a cello teacher and performer to translate Mantel's book into English. Once I had begun the job, however, I discovered that each new chapter I translated from the German was providing me with invaluable concepts and terminology to use in my day-to-day teaching routine. This daily interaction between teaching cello and translating *Cello Technique* not only contributed to my teaching but also helped the translation, for it clarified, through application, many hypotheses put forward in the book.

In presenting a wealth of objective information the author to a large extent avoids the controversies existing between different schools of cello playing. So, while it is not a method as such, *Cello Technique* covers the ground that is the indispensable basis on which any sound method must be built. It is the only attempt since Hugo Becker's *Mechanik und Ästhetik des Violoncellospiels* to relate in a systematic way the sciences of anatomy and physics to the technical problems of cello playing. By presenting *Cello Technique* in English, I have endeavored to share with my English-speaking colleagues this source of valuable teaching and study materials.

Some changes have been made in translation by the author and the translator for clarification of salient points in the original text. Liberties were taken with the original manuscript where text material seemed inappropriate for an English edition.

BARBARA HAIMBERGER THIEM

AMES, IOWA

INTRODUCTION

This book is not meant to be a "cello method." There are several good recently published instruction books that effectively outline the progression from simple to more complicated problems of cello technique. They provide guides for the teacher and practice material for the student designed to build up technique systematically, and they usually also contain instructions as to posture, practicing methods, and standards of perfection. What these books have in common is that they describe the *process* of learning from the first hesitant attempts to the more or less independent state of technical proficiency, and thus they have an important place in the pedagogy of our instrument.

Works that deal with the following question are rarer: *What actually happens when one plays an instrument?* These works attempt to appraise the player's technique at a given point in his development. The question should not be what stage of development the player has reached but what does a proficient player do *differently* from a less-proficient player? (The less-proficient player and the proficient player may be the same person before and after a practicing session.)

Characteristic of the first approach (which looks at the process of learning) is: Practice this passage until you master it. Characteristic of the second approach (which looks at the causes of success or failure) is: Try to observe what *happens* when you play a certain passage perfectly as opposed to when you play it poorly.

Although no one can skip certain phases of development (everyone must go through a learning process), we will concentrate on the second approach in this book. Since this approach is possible and meaningful at any stage in the learning process, it does not offer an instruction method in the strict sense. Of course, it presupposes a certain basic knowledge of the cello, but it can provide any cellist, teacher, student, or self-taught player (and to a certain extent everyone is self-taught) with practice suggestions regardless of the player's stage of development.

The suggestions are based on the experience that practicing without an accurate idea of *what* needs to be practiced is a waste of time. This idea seems obvious, but it becomes more significant when we ask the question: Which aspect of playing technique are we practicing right now? Rhythm? Intonation? Memory? Sound quality? Tempo? Conceptual precision? Phrasing? Coordination of left and right? Examination of body tensions? Elegance of movement? Energy and perseverance? We have a choice of many aspects. Naturally it is impossible to concentrate on all of them at once. In a good practicing session only a few are considered at a time.

If a central idea is lacking in his practicing the player will make no progress and may actually do damage, for everything that prevents the successful playing of a passage will through frequent repetition become automatic. Finally the passage will be completely automatic—but wrong.

Some instructions that may be relevant in a certain context can become false when generalized. They may lead to a dead end with no easy way out. Often they are based on inexact observations, on the confusion of position (which is static) with movement (which is dynamic), or simply on the uncritical acceptance of traditional instructions handed down from teacher to teacher. Here are some examples of such imprecise instructions:

The left thumb should touch the neck of the cello *loosely.*
The right arm should be held *low* (or *high*).
Play *forte* with *all* the hair of the bow, *piano* with *part* of it.
In a shift the arm must *fall* into the next position.
The right thumb should be *relaxed.*

This list could be extended indefinitely. But instructions that cannot be explained do not give the student the opportunity to gain experience through his own insight into the usefulness of these instructions or the opportunity to practice and finally to perfect that which he himself recognizes as appropriate.

A book about cello technique encounters one basic difficulty: We must somehow differentiate between the realm of music and the realm of technique. From the standpoint of the player's sensations we cannot divide cello playing into physical, emotional, and mental categories, with technique referring to the physical one. It is obvious that a deficient technique hinders musical expression, since a beautiful artistic concept is lost if it is not transformed into sound. Deficient technique corrupts the resulting sound, and even an imaginative player's concept of the result will be limited if he does not have at his disposal the means to render convincingly the smallest details of phrasing. In addition, physical strain, combined with constant disappointment, eventually creates a state of frustration that precludes an authoritative artistic rendering. Conversely, technical control of one's playing stimulates the search for ever new expressive shadings.

Thus technique cannot be separated from the experience of making music. It is possible, however, to divide the complete process of playing into logical sections that can be learned and taught separately. For practical purposes we can separate "technique" from "interpretation" and at the same time obtain a point of departure for the analysis of this technique.

Such an analysis might be outlined as follows:

1. The personality of the player, with all the imagination, energy, feeling, and knowledge available to him, sets the standards.

2. This personality creates a *musical concept* of the desired results.

3. To realize this concept the player needs detailed knowledge of the demands of the instrument, i.e., insight (possibly intuitive) into the necessary relationship between the sound and its physical production.

4. The body must have the physical ability to transform these demands into movement, i.e., the instrument has to be handled with the necessary strength and flexibility.

5. These three factors, musical concept, physical conditioning, and the demands of the instrument, lead to the *goal conception.* This conception includes the position on the fingerboard and the preconceived pitch. It is also based on memory of the requisite movement. For the left hand this goal conception anticipates the end of the movement, while for the right it controls the course of the movement.

6. In turn, the goal conception initiates movement. The goal can, however, be attained with different movements.

7. Certain *motor sensations,* which can be more or less distinct, accompany each movement.

8. These sensations exercise a steady *control* over the movement by comparing it continuously (unconsciously) with the goal conception and by correcting it.

9. Goal conception, movement, and sensation form an interrelated *control complex.* The continually correcting impulses that control the external movement are influenced by minimal psychic tensions as well. Put another way, the tensions are the internal equivalent of what happens externally (physiologically). They

mirror the effects of hope and disappointment. (N.B.: The continual correction is not a correction of the pitch but of the movement itself, even *before* the pitch is reached.)

10. The movement finally produces sound.

11. Another control mechanism, the ear, compares the sound result with the musical concept and again influences the goal conception of the movement.

A graphic outline of the process, shown below, seems very

physical conditions   demands of the instrument   musical concept

control by comparison   → goal conception ←   control by comparison

motor sensations ←——→ movement

sound ——————→ listening

theoretical, but it leads to practical considerations for influencing the learning process:

1. Musical demands cannot be executed unless the muscles are trained to be ready for active movement.

2. Misconceptions about the conditions of sound production prohibit a correction; if the conception and the actual execution of a movement do not match, external and internal tensions will result.

3. An imprecise goal conception cannot produce a precise movement.

4. An inefficient physical movement requires an unnecessary expenditure of energy and, as will be explained later, decreases the possibilities for control.

5. An imprecise motor sensation cannot yield precise control information or send out precise correcting impulses.

Instead of merely polishing the end results, we must examine each of these principles to see how they can lead to more perfect playing.

The playing *experience* is a unit. Although each hand has different functions, their cooperation cannot be split into "left" and "right." A mistake sensed in one arm will influence the other; an ideal movement in one arm makes a similar one easier in the other. We can even say that an ideal movement is only possible and sensed as such if it includes both arms, for any movement influences the equilibrium of the entire body and requires unconscious muscle tensions to maintain the balanced state or to regain it. The muscles involved in one arm may in turn be responsible for movement in the other.

A movement follows the demands of the extremities, i.e., of the fingers; the finger movements, however, are only the last instance of a series of muscle movements that are coordinated in the center of the body. The coordination is best if the actions of the two arms never disturb the equilibrium of the body, not even in a sudden motion. We do not always notice such disturbances because the body is stabilized by reflex reactions.

The principle that a goal-directed total movement is the basis of a virtuoso technique can be demonstrated best by studying the central problem of the position change, which we will deal with at the beginning of the second part of this book. In the first part we will discuss the general characteristics of movement.

CELLO TECHNIQUE

Part One

GOAL-DIRECTED MOVEMENT

I

ON CONTROLLING
MOVEMENT

General Issues

TO FIND forms of movement that meet the demands of the cello,
we must examine the mechanism of a goal-directed body movement and look for ways of manipulating the process of learning
such movements.

Any body movement is based on the following scheme:

1. We conceive a goal. This conception may be visually or
acoustically determined, or it may be derived from our *movement
memory.**

2. The brain sends motor impulses through the nerve pathways to the muscles. We need not go into the physiological details
of those nerve pathways, except to say that each motor impulse
consists of a series of pointlike single impulses. The frequency of
the impulses and the number of muscle fibres involved determine
the amplitude and the force of the movement, respectively.

3. A second system of nerve pathways reports success or failure to the brain, i.e., whether the goal was reached (feedback). In

---

* The term *movement memory* is used to describe the ability to remember
and repeat a certain movement.

response the brain sends out correcting impulses. Their success or failure is also reported to the brain. We must imagine this circuit in uninterrupted activity.

The most obvious comparison for such a control mechanism is driving a car: The driver looks at the street, notices a slight change in direction, and makes a correcting movement with the steering wheel. He determines the correcting movement according to the extent of the discrepancy. The comparison can be taken still further: A beginner, seeing the car heading for the ditch, will turn the wheel sharply in the opposite direction. Then just before the car moves into the left lane, he will jerk the wheel to the right again, straight toward the next tree. This game will continue back and forth. An experienced driver, by contrast, will make only minimal adjustments when driving straight ahead.

Let us look at this control mechanism as it applies to the cello. To play an octave shift on one string, one first imagines the pitch acoustically and then slides toward it on the fingerboard. At the moment the pitch is reached, the ear will report this fact to the brain, which in turn will inform the muscles that the movement must be stopped.

In his *Kunst des Violinspiels* (The Art of Violin Playing), Carl Flesch starts from this idea of acoustic control and adds the demand that the finger quickly and continually correct any out-of-tune pitch on the spot. This demand seems only reasonable, at first glance. Let us ignore for now the aesthetic problems of intonation—there are a number of exhaustive studies on the subject (e.g., Christine Heman, *Intonation auf Streichinstrumenten* [Intonation on String Instruments], Baerenreiter, 1964) —and let us assume that the pitch is imagined, regardless of the intonation system. According to this acoustic control system anyone with a good ear should be able to play absolutely in tune after having practiced how to correct instantly. Experience, however, shows that this is not the case. By the time the player has noticed an out-of-tune pitch the attentive listener has observed it too. A control mechanism based on only the heard sound therefore works too slowly to guarantee a precise intonation.

It is incomprehensible to many interested amateurs that a player with an indisputably good ear will stay on an out-of-tune pitch for some time. It is, in fact, remarkable how much time passes before an inexact pitch is corrected; in fact, the correcting movement often goes too far in the opposite direction and produces another inexact pitch. We therefore have to admit that the ear gives the final confirmation of right and wrong, but it is too cumbersome to be the center of control during the movement itself, i.e., too much time passes between the original movement and the correcting movements demanded by the ear. We therefore have to find a different center of control for the movement.

Through frequent practicing the body acquires a movement memory and manages to store quite precise information on any motor experience. This experience is defined by the pitch it aims for, but it includes the entire physical process from any anticipating movements to the final configuration of the hand. There is no time for a correction when the heard sound is compared to the actual goal of the movement; the process is finished before it can be checked. But there is time for a correction while the movement in process and the movement memory are being compared. Since the movement is perceived as an entirety, deviations from it can be noticed and corrected before success or failure has been decided. Therefore we must try to start the movement relatively early before reaching the final pitch.

We can make another comparison with driving a car: If the driver steers the car directly toward the goal without correcting until he realizes that he has ended up several feet to the right of his goal and then shifts into reverse and steers for the goal once more, it takes him considerably longer to reach it than if he makes corrections long before he arrives. Such anticipatory movements will be described in detail later.

Now we have to go one step further: Psychological experiments have proven that even the *conception* of a movement will send out through the nerve pathways minimal electric impulses that do not actually cause movement in the limbs but prepare their action. This means that even before any movement is visible, the circuit in the control mechanism has begun. Thus the *anticipated* pattern of movement can be compared to the *movement memory* and can be provisionally corrected.

However, the anticipatory sensation of a movement is dependent on the conception of its goal. Without a clear conception of the goal, no unambiguous motor sensation will be formed with regard to the goal; without the latter no clear patterns develop for the movement memory.

The process of the movement is dictated by the goal conception. In order to pick up an object one's movements must be coordinated so as to achieve that result. The control mechanism is active in each part of this movement; in this case it is controlled by the eye. If one looks at an object, closes one's eyes, and then picks it up, the precision will be slightly reduced, but, considering that the eyes are closed, still surprisingly high. In this case an internal, quasi-visual conception of the object dictates the process of the movement. Even then the previous control mechanism is at work.

If the movement memory is employed as an additional means of control, the precision will be considerably higher. If one repeatedly reaches for an object with eyes closed, always using the same movement, after a few tries he will hit the target accurately every time. If we change the position of the object or of the person, when he looks at the object, closes his eyes, and reaches for it again, he will be less precise until his movement memory is activated by repeating the movement several times. Repetition builds the movement pattern in the memory.

Thus we can conclude that an important precondition for the precision of a movement is a sharp conception. The ear has such a sharp conception but can only correct when the process of the movement has come to an end. Therefore we cannot call the ear a control center in the strict sense of a controlling mechanism.

Goal Conception

When we refer to a goal-directed movement we are mainly concerned with the accuracy of the left hand. The movement of the right arm is also in a certain sense goal-directed, but the conception is less important for it. Acoustic control is possible during all phases of the right-arm movement. For the left arm, however, acoustic control is only possible when the entire movement has come to an end. This means that the actual control of the movement must take place in the realm of conception.

Thus we must face the fact that conceptual ability determines the accuracy of intonation. Conceptual ability may refer to the realm of sound as well as to the realm of space (the fingerboard). In order to achieve maximal conceptual precision we must look at both realms separately right now. Let us suppose that a player has enough musical judgment to be able to tell whether an interval is in tune when he *hears* it, but, as was pointed out before, the subsequent acoustic control comes too late to be of any help during the actual movement.

If, however, a musician attempts to "hear" the exact pitch of a tone *before it sounds,* he will have to concede that the precision of this conception varies greatly, even if the nature of the interval is perfectly clear. Since the movement can at best be only as exact as the goal conception, we must force ourselves while practicing to

postpone a movement until we can envision the desired pitch un-
ambiguously.

The conceptual ability of the ear can be trained considerably.
Many string players are under the illusion that their ears are
sufficiently developed since the concept of an interval is clear to
them and since they can judge the pitch of a *heard* interval. We
must emphasize once more that we are not concerned with the
concept of a third or a seventh but with the actual pitch, unam-
biguously envisioned by the ear.

This pitch has an exact equivalent on the fingerboard. We
therefore have to train not only the acoustic precision of the conception but also the corresponding spatial precision, for even more
certainty. After practicing both elements, the spatial conception
will soon be coordinated with the acoustic one to the extent that
a precise acoustic conception will initiate a precise spatial conception as a reflex. Finally the acoustic (musical) conception will
be almost enough to cause an essentially unconscious process of
movement that leads to the goal.

How can we train such a quasi-visual, spatial goal conception?
If one looks at an object and then closes one's eyes the object will
still be present in the imagination; the inner visual precision will,
however, diminish after a while. If one has to imagine an object
one has not seen before, for example, a black dot, one has difficulty
doing so with closed eyes; the shape, the blackness, and the location on the visual field are quite vague. With concentration and
practice the precision of the conception can be increased.

Walter Gieseking is reported to have said that he could not
play even a very easy piece of music with absolute certainty. Coming from a man like Gieseking, who possessed phenomenal imaginative powers, such an utterance seems surprising. He is said to
have learned music by memory by merely looking at it. If, however, one considers that any precise conception will always have

certain insecure spots and that any movement, even the seemingly easiest, only reaches its goal through a series of mostly unconscious correcting impulses, we have to admire Giescking's self-observation.

On the fingerboard we have no visible marks which would facilitate aiming for and hitting the right pitch. As string players we are dependent on the development of our conceptual abilities from the start. In this context conceptual ability means the capacity to fix a location on the fingerboard quasi-visually so that it becomes the unmistakable local goal of a movement.

It has been suggested that beginners mark the chromatic notes on the fingerboard with horizontal lines in order to facilitate "geographic" orientation. However, we do not want to rely on the eyes when searching for a pitch but must imagine clear marks on the fingerboard without visual help. We therefore suggest the following practicing aid:

Draw the fingerboard on a piece of paper and mark all chromatic notes (for about two and a half octaves) as horizontal lines. For better orientation mark important intervals, especially octaves, fifths, and fourths, perhaps in different colors, so that the various intervals can be distinguished easily. Hang this schematic version of the fingerboard about three feet in front of you during practice sessions. Now fix the location of every sound visually on the control fingerboard before playing it.

This method has several important advantages, but, of course, it cannot solve all our problems.

1. The location can be seen distinctly with the eye. Each place on the fingerboard has a visible equivalent and a distinct contour.

2. The distances between the notes and their relationship to one another become clear. In addition to the movement memory,

visual control, which in our everyday life regulates most of our movements and which otherwise would not be utilized at all, is introduced.

3. We are forced to become aware of every sound and its position within the chromatic system. It will not do simply to play a sequence of intervals without consciously realizing the absolute pitch of the individual sounds. This exercise corresponds to the solfège, which is practiced in France. The use of our schematic fingerboard accomplishes more than the solfège in this case since the latter makes us aware only of the abstract positions, but does not present their equivalents on the fingerboard.

4. With this method we have to become aware of *each* pitch separately. Often we look in the wrong place for the reason why a certain passage does not work. We can localize the difficulty, but the cause might well be found before or after the suspected passage. In a fast passage, for instance, often a finger is put down and a little later is used for a position change. If the second function is not anticipated in the first action and the finger is only taken along unconsciously, the position change is bound to fail.

5. In each case the conception of the sound and the place has to precede the actual movement. *Conception* in this context means anticipation. We will explain in detail later why playing a sequence of fast notes is basically different from a fast playing of a sequence of slow notes. In fast passages the individual movements are combined into one movement pattern; that is not the case in a slow passage. Only a timely anticipation of all the notes makes it possible to turn the individual movements into a total movement pattern. If one note is missing in this conscious anticipation there will be a discrepancy between the conception of the movement and the acoustically desired results. This discrepancy will immediately result in a tightness. If the course of the movement is not anticipated in time, no compound movement pattern will be formed

and the movement will adjust with great difficulty to the note-by-note demands.

The limits of this proposed method are obvious.

1. We can practice only very slowly since faster passages escape the analytic abilities of the eye. However, in this case we are not practicing fluency but pitch consciousness. Indirectly this "geographic" pitch consciousness will eventually help fluency also, since a clear conception of the individual pitches is also vital for fluency.

2. This method is extremely exhausting; half an hour's practicing requires immense concentration. However, this kind of practicing will bring obvious and immediate results; that is not always the case after several hours of "hit or miss" practicing.

3. The final shape of the movement, i.e., assembling the various individual movements into a compound motion, cannot be practiced with this method. But often the tensions that occur are not the result of an incorrect movement but merely of a vague conception of the goal.

An insecure conception and the resulting fear of failure create muscle tensions that affect the arm during crucial moments in the actual movement and thereby change the whole pattern of muscle activity. As a result the movement memory is jeopardized, since it remembers a different muscle pattern from that which is necessary when the additional tensions are included. Still more insecurity results, creating a vicious circle that the player himself is often not aware of.

4. This method is only applicable when playing by memory. Training a visual conception of the fingerboard, though, will eventually help sight-reading also; in this exercise reading a note stimulates not only a reflex conception of the interval and of the position but also of the individual "frets" on the fingerboard.

A precise goal conception can be improved still further. So far we have divided the fingerboard into clearly visible or imagined "frets." These "frets" should not be drawn or imagined too wide, since they would leave too much latitude for the conception of the individual note. Since the tip of the finger is much wider than a "fret," even if the finger hits right on such a "fret" there will still be some space between the lower and upper edges of its contact area. This distance is, of course, far too large to guarantee a clean intonation. In addition to training our conception of the fingerboard, we have to narrow down the width of the finger in our imagination so that it will correspond to the imagined width of the "fret." This means that we have to imagine not a contact *area* but a contact *line,* which runs perpendicular to the string exactly in the middle of the contact area. The direction in which the finger strikes the string is determined by the middle axis of the finger, and the sensation of movement and pressure refer to this middle axis.

We will leave it up to the reader to find his own way of envisioning this idea. You may imagine that the finger is only a fraction of an inch wide, or that the finger tips are wedge-shaped, or that you are playing on the bones—the result will be the same. Your conception will be sharpened as though you were looking at the final goal of your movement through a magnifying glass.

Control of Movement

Let us remember for a moment that we are looking for ways to increase the precision of a movement. The movement memory is not sufficient by itself; in addition a precise goal conception is needed for every individual movement. The precision of this conception can be increased. We should not imagine, however, that the movement memory is a finished model that will inevitably result in the exact repetition of an already imprinted process.

Otherwise we could not explain how a position change will work repeatedly, and, then, at the moment when it really counts, will fail. Instead we have to picture the movement memory as the sum of experiences collected through frequent repetitions of one movement—the relationship between the motor sensations involved and the success of the movement. Thus we do not recall the finished pattern of a movement. Rather, *the relationship between the motor sensations and the success of the movement (stored as experience in the movement memory) leads to different movement patterns according to the goal conception and the initial position on the instrument.*

Let us use the example of an automobile once more. Even a good driver cannot drive into his own garage with his eyes closed. However, it is no problem for him to drive into a strange, narrow garage with his eyes open. His experience has not taught him in detail which movements of the steering wheel are necessary, but he has learned what effect a certain turn of the steering wheel will have on the direction of the car. In this analogy, seeing the garage corresponds to imagining the musical goal. Knowing the relationship between the steering wheel and the direction the car will take is equivalent to knowing the relationship between the motor sensations and the success of a particular movement on the cello.

Here is another example: A good violinist, after a short period of adjustment, will play the viola much better than a violist who is not as good a player. This will be true even though the violist has had many chances to memorize the necessary motor sensations for intervals on the viola. Thus the superiority of the good violinist cannot be based on a memory of finished patterns of movement. His superiority results from his better association of motor sensations and successful movements. However, we do not want to maintain that there is no such thing as an absolute memory of certain motor sensations; at first the good violinist in our example will play less in tune on the viola than on his violin. But we might question whether that is not due in part to his goal conception rather than to a possibly invalid movement memory. In any case, we can say that the common principle of repeatedly drilling a passage does not get to the heart of the matter. Any practicing method based on such an assumption will lead to disappointment.

As we explained before, a continuous flow of sensations reports success or failure of the movements. The finer the differences in muscle tensions the player can sense the more precisely the correcting impulses will work. Below a certain minimum the differences no longer register. We can also put it this way: A certain threshold of sensitivity has to be passed before a correction is possible at all. The lower this threshold the better the movement can be controlled. One of the decisive questions in the art of movement therefore is: What factors determine the height of this threshold? If one lifts two full buckets consecutively, one cannot tell whether one of them contains five grams more water than the other. If five grams (less than ¼ ounce) of water is poured into a small glass, one can detect immediately that it is heavier than it was before. In the first case a lot of energy is needed to lift the bucket; it would take considerably more than five grams to make a noticeable difference. In the second case, when the muscles need to lift only the slight weight of the glass, the few additional grams become evident. In the first case the threshold is high; in the second it is low. Therefore we can deduce the following: In a state of low muscle tension a smaller *difference* in muscle tension will be registered than in a state of high muscle activity.

This problem has been examined by psychologists. Weber and Fechner's Law states that the proportion between a given muscle tension and the minimum addition that is realized as different is approximately constant. E. H. Weber established that for lifting weights the threshold is about 1/40 of the initial weight. For 40 grams it is 1 gram; for 40 kilograms, 1 kilogram.

More recent tests have established that a moving limb will have a considerably lower threshold than a fixed one. H. Rohracher mentions in his *Einführung in die Psychologie* (Introduction to Psychology) that the threshold of a muscle will fluctuate between 1/3 of the initial weight (with taut muscle) and 1/200 (with a passively moving limb, as in throwing underhand). These data themselves are not of interest to us but they have decisive implications for our study:

1. The lower the muscle tension, the more precise the feedback and the control.

2. Limbs in motion can be controlled more precisely than fixed limbs.

This leads us to the problem of muscle relaxation, which we will have to examine in still greater detail. It is no use simply to limit the amount of energy we use. Instead we have to try to keep all the muscles involved in a certain movement at the lowest possible level of tension. But before we can apply the term *relaxation* in a meaningful way, we must examine the influence of mass and energy on a movement.

II

THE PHYSICS
OF MOVEMENT

Energy and Mass

ANY movement in the body results from the shortening of a muscle. We are used to regarding this mechanism as a change in the position of a mobile part of the body in relation to a fixed one closer to the center of the body. Looking at such a muscle contraction closely, we notice that shortening the muscle only changes the angle between the two bones of the joint. Both bones thus experience an equally strong force, but in opposite directions. Since the weight of the peripheral bone is less than that of the rest of the body, a visible movement occurs in the peripheral bone of the joint. The force affecting the bone closer to the body, however, is just as great. Through a sudden muscle contraction the bone closer to the body receives a jolt, which can be counteracted or balanced by some muscle action in a different part of the body.

There is still more involved in a simple movement of one joint. A muscle contraction generates energy, which causes an acceleration of the moving bone of the joint. As long as the muscle energy is effective, the acceleration continues, i.e., the speed increases. If the speed is not to increase further, the energy causing it must be stopped. At this point, the inertia of the mass of the moving bone maintains the speed as long as no resistance (external or internal friction, air) slows it down. To diminish the speed or to stop the movement some force must be employed in a direction opposite to the initial one. This means that the antagonist of the originally active muscle must be used.

An activation of the antagonist causes another jolt to the bone closer to the body, this time in the direction opposite to the initial one. Therefore, in a jerky motion, we can clearly discern two jolts going through the body segments and causing a considerable concussion of the body. The force of the concussion depends on the degree of acceleration or deceleration of the involved mass. Let us keep in mind that this concussion of the trunk is not initiated by any of the trunk muscles. It is therefore a passive body movement.

A passive movement may also be created in the opposite direction, from the center of the body toward the periphery. A jerky active twist of the trunk causes a rather large arm motion if the arm musculature is relaxed. This motion extends through the shoulders, upper arms, and forearms to the hands. The visible movement of the hand and fingers is again not caused by any of the hand and finger muscles.

There is a third kind of passive movement, one that is initiated in a different place or at an earlier time. The elasticity of the body or of its parts causes a limb to bounce back passively to its more relaxed state. A trunk motion to the right therefore is followed by an elastic motion back into the normal position as soon as all the trunk muscles relax again.

We see now that a motion of the body or its parts is not necessarily indicative of the existence and the direction of muscular activity. The movement may be under the influence of muscle contraction or it may be in the subsequent phase after the muscle activity has ceased. It may be in a slowing-down phase or in a rebounding phase, depending on the body material involved.

So far we have looked at the muscles only in their relation to movement. The second task of the muscles is to maintain a certain posture of the body. Here the muscles do not initiate movement, but hinder it by giving appropriate resistance to external forces. When an arm is extended horizontally, the muscles must work to maintain this position by counteracting the force of gravity. The movement starts only as soon as the muscles stop working. Gravity, however, is not the only external force that the muscles have to balance with support activity. The momentum of a moving limb is such an external force. If the forearm and hand are to be moved at the elbow without a movement of the wrist, an additional force must be active in the wrist to prevent the hand from being tossed further. If the forearm is moved back and forth, the flexing and extending muscles of the wrist will have to be used alternately so that no additional hand movement results.

Similarly, when continuous pressure is exerted by the finger on the fingerboard or the bow on the string, no movement in the direction of the pressure results. Rather the musculature of one limb (e.g., the finger) offers adequate resistance to the pressure exercised by the limb closer to the body (the hand), so that the position remains unchanged. The muscle energy used to maintain a certain position must be the exact equivalent of the external force (gravity, momentum, force of a different limb).

If, in a muscle pair, the antagonist were completely relaxed, the entire energy of the agonist would be available for the movement or for the exertion of pressure. However, a complete relaxation of any one muscle is impossible. A certain amount of tension exists even if the muscle feels completely relaxed. If both muscles, flexor and extensor, are activated, the force moving the joint is only as great as the difference in force of the two muscles. If the flexor and the extensor are strongly activated, only a small effective difference remains for use. The same effective difference could be produced with much less tension in both muscles. Even though in the first case movement is still possible, the sensitivity threshold for small differences of activation is raised, as we saw before, and fine control over the muscle activity is lessened.

Equilibrium

We have seen that maintaining a certain position of a joint requires muscle work. So does the equilibrium of the whole body. Gravity will pull down even the seated body if the static equilibrium is changed ever so slightly. If the equilibrium is disturbed from without, there are two possibilities for correction:

1. The body may shift its center of gravity and thus restore its equilibrium in a new posture.

2. Muscles that will have a stabilizing influence may be activated.

Regaining equilibrium by changing the posture of the body requires one single movement but little or no muscle activity to maintain it. Therefore a change of posture is preferable to muscle support.

When the center of gravity is in the middle axis of the chest, no force must operate in either direction; gravity pulls at all points evenly and equilibrium is maintained. The basic posture at the cello therefore should be one where the chest is not tilted to either side, front or back. The nervous system normally prevents loss of balance, and maintaining it occurs unconsciously, but we can nonetheless influence the kind of correction. It is important that the body be ready to move at all times. A flexible body will react with an adequate change of posture, while in an inflexible one, the correction will be achieved by muscle stiffening.

The equilibrium may be disturbed by:

1. A jolt. We have seen that abrupt movements send a jolt through the entire body. While it may not be sufficient to knock

the body over, the jolt might shake its base at a decisive moment and thereby endanger a goal-directed body movement from its very inception. Abrupt motions, therefore, tend to jeopardize exactness, especially when a position change is involved.

2. A shift of weight. Most movements during playing involve a shift of weight. Every whole-bow stroke and every position change shifts the center of gravity of the body and necessitates small corrections in posture.

There are some movements within the body that do not disturb the equilibrium—those in which two equal masses move in opposite directions. They occur wherever a limb is turned around its own axis. A rotation of the entire spine does not entail a disturbance of the equilibrium either, since it is also a balanced shift of weight. The center of gravity remains unchanged, no matter which point of rotation the spine is at.

It may also happen that several limbs form a mobile system in which two masses in contrary motion neutralize the effects of jolts and shifts of weight. The hand and forearm constitute such a system when the hand moves up and down quickly at the wrist: when the hand moves down, the wrist and forearm move up. The forearm and upper arm form another system if the arm is flexed and extended quickly at the elbow: the forearm flexes at the elbow, the upper arm moves back. If the elbow's location is fixed, however, the force exerted (by actively preventing an otherwise passive upper-arm movement) and the concussion of the body are considerably higher. The double lever is another such system (see p. 192).

We see now that the entire body is involved even in a simple movement. Goal-directed movements, however, are generally composed of many individual movements. Hence we can hardly find out about the actual force relationships in a total body movement by concentrating on the individual functions of a joint.

Muscle tightness in any playing motion may have two basically different causes:

1. The movement requires too much force in relation to its purpose (e.g., shift of a finger), since it is put together impractically. In this case we have to apply a different movement, i.e., a movement which uses different muscle groups (e.g., double lever instead of a whole-arm motion).

2. The form of the movement is purposeful but it is executed with too much prior fixation of the involved joints. This cause is harder to remedy, since it is frequently combined with psychological tensions. Some of the following suggestions may help in this case: tension-reducing exercises away from the instrument, a longer break, sleep, breathing exercises, analysis of the movement in time, sharpening of the goal-conception.

Energy Reserve and Looseness

Although it is necessary to keep muscle activity at a minimum, it does not follow that vigorous playing does not require much strength. As we saw, the acceleration and speed of a limb depend on its mass and the available strength. We cannot influence the mass of a limb; we can, however, prevent the involvement of unnecessary masses. To achieve a strong sound at the tip of the bow, the applied force of the rotation of the forearm (pronation) and of the stiffened index finger may well tap the energy reserves of the player. The left hand also needs great strength for fast movements when the string has to be pressed firmly to the fingerboard for each individual note. Intensive vibrato also requires strength. In those cases neither better movements nor concentration on greater looseness will help. Since the tiring of the muscles depends on the available energy reserves, a player with weak muscles will be able to execute movements requiring great strength for a short time only.

To prevent such exhaustion, he will not use the full potential of his strength, and his playing as a whole will be weak.

The applied force is noticeable, first of all, in the *pressure* on the bow and in the pressure of the fingers on the fingerboard. But the *speed* (more precisely, the acceleration) of a movement also depends on the amount of force applied: In the right arm, a fast détaché uses much strength; in the fingers of the left hand, the speed and therefore the preciseness of the attack are in direct proportion to the available strength.

Flexibility is also indirectly dependent on the energy reserves: The smaller the energy reserves (i.e., the available energy not in use) the greater the effort demanded by a certain work output.

1. If we come close to tapping the energy reserves, exhaustion is bound to occur soon.

2. The stronger a muscle is tensed in proportion to its maximum capacity the more time it will need afterwards to relax again.

3. During great strain, the danger arises that disturbing innervations* of other muscles (cramps) will develop.

How can the playing musculature be strengthened? Intensive practicing, of course, strengthens it to a certain extent. The purpose of most exercises and etudes, however, is not to strengthen muscles but to develop coordination of movement. In normal playing we rarely use all our energy reserves. Therefore a player will hardly blame a technical failure on his lack of strength. However, the greater the energy reserve the greater the energy available for playing without strain; the relation between the two stays the same. To increase the energy available without strain it is necessary to increase the energy reserves. Therefore we have to find exercises that reach the limits of the player's strength. He can push the limit further only if he reaches it again and again.

* Innervation: The amount of nerve stimulation received by a part of the body.

Here we might apply a term used in sports: Record perform-
ances in sports are achieved with "interval training." In this kind
of training, the limits of one's capacity are approached again and
again, interrupted by periods of rest when the strained muscles can
recover. The purpose of such exercises is not to control the process
of movement but to repeat an exercise until exhaustion sets in.
We notice that when doing such exercises on the cello (e.g., double
trill exercises), strength as well as control decrease in the process.
If the exercises are continued, the movement pattern often collapses even before the flexibility of the finger suffers.

When the muscle tires, the effort, i.e., the expenditure of
energy in relation to the energy reserves, has to become greater to
achieve the minimum requirements of the intrument. Even strong,
well-trained muscles will show a decrease in performance, although
it will take longer for them to tire.

Special demands are made on the following muscles: the
fingers of the left hand, the wrist, the index finger of the right
hand, and the rotatory muscles of the forearm. The rotatory
muscles of the left upper arm are also strained if one vibrates
intensely.

Isometric exercises are one possibility for strengthening those
muscles *directly*. An isometric contraction of a muscle means an
increase in the muscle tension without movement, i.e., exerting
pressure against a firm object. In these exercises the limb in question is pressed against a resisting object for about 10 seconds with
a great effort (but not maximum effort). As a consequence the
muscle fibres, which are usually not used, will be activated, and
individual muscle fibres will be strengthened by repeated usage.
The fingers may be pressed against a table top. The rotatory
muscles of the forearm may be exercised by attempting to break
a strong stick held horizontally with both hands. These exercises
should be used with caution, however. In this form they should
not be done more than once or twice a day; overstraining

incurs the danger of inflammation of the ligaments or of other damage.

From sports medicine we have learned that isometric exercises increase the strength but not the speed of a muscle function (if we disregard the *indirect* effect on the flexibility obtained by lessening the strain). Their direct effect is limited to increasing the mere pressure function of the limb when in continuous use. They are very appropriate for the fingers of the left hand, which tend to tire too quickly when playing long sustained notes. After a few weeks of isometric exercises there will be a considerable increase in the strength of the involved muscles, possibly doubling the original strength (as can be checked with scales).

To train the *speed* itself isotonic exercises are recommended. They combine an even strain on the muscles with a movement of the involved joints. For example, the flexed fingers press evenly on a table while the hand moves up and down. The flexibility of the wrist can be trained by doing the same movement against the resistance of the other hand. The flexibility of the forearm rotation is increased by pressing one fist against the palm of the other hand and turning it back and forth against this friction. The reader can easily find the most appropriate exercises for himself.

It is important that one use about $\frac{2}{3}$ of the available energy; if less is used there will be no improvement of the involved muscles. These exercises must be done with considerable exertion with respect to both energy and endurance until a noticeable tiring sets in, but not, however, until one reaches a state of exhaustion. Practicing scales for hours cannot serve this cause, as we have well realized; it is illusory to believe that the amount of time devoted to technique in this way will bring further technical advantages, once the "image" pattern of the scale has been established.

III

MOVEMENT AS *GESTALT*

Movement in Space

WE HAVE seen that even a simple movement in one joint has its effect on the rest of the body: jolts, disturbances of the equilibrium, automatic corrections, and resilience. Any goal-directed body movement, however, consists of a combination of various partial movements, which are organized in a unified *gestalt*. This coordination should not be viewed as the sum of learned individual movements. We do not learn clearly circumscribed movements that we can reproduce exactly and can put together as needed. Instead we have to understand the goal-directed body movement as an entirety dictated by its goal. Here is an analogy: The conception has the effect of a magnetic field, which organizes the iron filings differently every time, but still in a similar overall pattern typical of that magnetic field.

The nervous system coordinates all phases of all partial movements according to the goal, including all physically necessary corrections. A movement therefore is carried out on the basis of trained coordinations, but is determined each time anew by its goal. Coordination thus does not imply that isolated movements are put together mechanically but refers to the production of the most purposeful pattern demanded by the situation. A goal thus can be reached with different combinations of movement: the exact reproduction of a movement in all its details is impossible in any case.

In his work *Allgemeine Theorie der menschlichen Haltung und Bewegung* (General Theory of Human Posture and Movement), J. J. Buitendyk mentions experimental tests in which the structure and the speed of the individual phases of an overhand throwing movement were measured accurately by using a high-speed camera. It was demonstrated that even when the ball was thrown repeatedly toward the same target, the accuracy of the throws varied less than did the partial movements leading to success. We therefore have to deduce that it is useless to try to memorize identical movement patterns while practicing. This was already clear when we saw that the external form of a movement is rarely indicative of the actual muscle activities taking place. Two completely identical-looking movements may be executed with muscle activity of different strengths or even with different muscle groups. If we cannot find the reason for the difference between exact and inexact movement and between success and failure in the external form of a movement, we have to look for different criteria.

We have seen that a movement executed with little effort can be controlled better than one using much muscle work, regardless of whether the extra muscle effort is the consequence of a cramp, i.e., of the simultaneous involvement of two opposed muscles (agonist and antagonist), or whether unnecessary parts are involved. More energy is expended to maintain a position than to execute a fluent movement that makes use of momentum. This means that a movement will be executed more accurately when fewer position fixations are used, i.e., when more of the joints participate in the movement process. Thus a fluent big movement may be more accurate than a choppy small one that uses only the absolutely indispensable joints and leaves the others fixed. What is functional because of its economy, control, and accuracy is also aesthetically graceful and harmonious (*harmonious*—Greek, put together). What looks good, sounds good.

The individual muscles of a movement *gestalt* are not sensed individually, but the sensation of the movement is again an entirety. It is difficult to correct a technically wrong movement (which is also sensed as an entirety) because the physical sensation itself has to be corrected. The position and the overfixation of the individual joints are also part of the total sensation. Such fixations can be tracked down only by close self-observation and eliminated with special exercises for the partial movements. Mere autosuggestion to "relax" does not open up any hitherto undiscovered possibilities for movement.

In order to organize the individual parts of the body into a complete and fluent movement all of them have to be ready to move at all times. If this readiness is lacking corrections of the equilibrium will be taken care of by tensions, which in turn diminish control. The shoulders and trunk must be kept especially ready for this reason. If the shoulder is not used to movement of its own it will hinder the course of a harmonious total movement. If the spine cannot flex torsionally it is not relaxed but lazy.

In addition, the information about the position of a limb, i.e., about the angle of a joint, is far more accurate when it is gained from a movement rather than from a rigid position. If someone places your completely relaxed left hand somewhere on the fingerboard, you will be able to determine its location only vaguely, and you may be several inches off. If, instead, the information about the location is derived from a movement, your mistake will be minimal.

If a joint stays rigid within a total movement it will transmit no information about its position. It is astonishing that even big body movements, especially of violinists, do not affect the intonation. The movement transmits maximum information about the position, as well as about the fingers. We can deduce from this that the principle of the greatest possible economy only applies to energy expenditure. It would be a basic misunderstanding to extend it to visible movement. A big visible movement may well require less strength than a smaller one. Including some not really "necessary" body movements may often be useful, since our aim is not primarily to use as little energy as possible but to get the most accurate results with the available energy. Buitendyk mentions an experiment in which a person is asked to point quickly at a specific object. On the first attempt the trunk must remain motionless. The next time it is allowed to move along. As a result the second movement was more accurate than the first. Thus, the principle of economy must be redefined as the principle of the least effort, independent of the work actually done.

Within the complicated processes of our neuromuscular system something else has to be taken into consideration: Innervation is influenced by psychological processes as well as by physical conditions; expressive movements may be uneconomical in the strict physical sense and still belong to the complete process; suppression of such movements may provoke an unwelcome tightness in a different place.

Since the innervations of compound movements happen homogeneously despite their complexity, stiffening at any one point in the total movement will cause stiffening, and even cramps, at another point. A stiff wrist tends to stiffen other muscle groups of the arm in turn. The tightness will even affect the opposite side of the body. Stiff leg muscles, as a consequence of a slippery floor or chair, may influence the entire movement negatively. All these processes can hardly be observed from without; every player has to control them for himself.

The only purpose of the playing motions of the entire body is to lead the fingers, its furthest extensions, to their required position. The fingers, so to speak, dictate how the rest of the body must move. The polarity between the fingers of the two hands produces the total body movement. Thus we must concentrate on this polarity. The physiological basis for it is the fact that the innervation of a limb on one side of the body sends out minimal innervations to the corresponding limb on the other side although they do not necessarily result in action. There is continuous communication between the nerves of the fingers of the two hands. Tightness in one hand will diminish the sensitivity of the other.

This principle can be proved with a simple experiment: Ask a person to make relaxed finger motions with both hands, and then suddenly ask him to make a fist with *one* hand. The relaxed finger motions of the *other* hand will also stop, in fact, it might tend to form a fist also. Even the well-trained hands of an instrumentalist will clearly show some of these effects.

If, during a shift of the left hand, the right hand is fixed in a specific position, the shift will be less secure than if flexibility of the right is maintained during the shift. One way to counteract this effect is to make a small movement with the fingers of the right hand during the shift or shortly before it. Try flexing and extending the knuckles* while making a contrary movement in the middle joints. The increase in sensitivity and control of the left hand will be surprising.

Experience teaches us that we can go one step further: The accuracy of a position change is determined not only by the final position of the finger but also by the angle at the wrist. By the same process, the sensitivity of the wrist can be improved by moving the right wrist a little before a position change by the left hand. If the position change happens to coincide with a bow change, merely emphasize the wrist movement of the bow change. If the position change occurs during the same bow the wrist move-

* Although all three joints of the finger are called "knuckles," for simplicity we will refer to the largest one, connecting the finger to the palm, as the "knuckle," and the other two as the "middle" and "last" joints, respectively.

ment should be that of the last bow change: For the position change on a down bow, the right hand turns slightly to the left (*adduction*); for the position change on an up bow, it turns slightly to the right (*abduction*). For the other joints of both arms the same left-right relationship holds true.

Exaggerating somewhat, we might say that the security of the left hand depends on the flexibility of all the joints of the right arm.

A beginner has to suppress the natural coordination of the two hands to start with: "The right hand should *not* know what the left hand is doing." In virtuoso playing, however, we are faced with the opposite situation. There are no movements by the separate halves of the body but only homogeneous movements determined by the fingers of both hands.

Movement in Time

Although the fingers dictate the movement, they do not start the series of body movements. The order of the various partial movements takes the opposite course, namely, toward the fingers. Normally the main energy for big movements is exerted by the trunk; the shoulders, upper arm, and forearm are moved along almost passively, while the hand and the fingers make the fine adjustments. We will see later that even passive movements of the trunk, initiated by active arm movements, may be used in such a way that the final movement will work almost passively and therefore have all the advantages with respect to expenditure of energy and control.

In another comparison, imagine a row of dominoes. If the first one is tipped over by an external force, each of the others will be pushed over by its neighbor. Even if a player believes that the chain of action starts at the extremity the order will not be reversed; instead the discrepancy between conception and execution will only result in a tense movement.

Neither should the realization that the movement proceeds toward the extremity lead us to overemphasizing the movement of the spine. The result would be a fixation at the extremity. Unnecessary fixation of the joints always affects the total movement, no matter whether this fixation is situated in the trunk or at the extremity.

The order of the partial movements reveals nothing about the *speed* of the process. Two principles apply here:

1. Great acceleration at the beginning requires great strength.
2. Maintaining a position requires strength.

For instance, if the arm is tossed out at great speed, little energy is required for maintaining the position, but the strong muscle contraction at the beginning of the movement lessens control. As we saw before, the initial movement and the sudden slowdown provoke innervations in different parts of the body, which compensate for the change. The jerkier the movement the stronger these innervations. In addition, the upper arm, when accelerated with a jerk, tends to innervate other parts of the arm and of the body even when no physical necessity exists. If, on the contrary, the arm is moved very slowly, no "tossing" phase results. Instead, energy for maintaining the position is needed during the entire movement.

Between these two extremes we must find the optimal speed of a movement. The acceleration must be gradual enough that it does not produce jolts that will require compensation; but it needs to be great enough that the main part of the movement will consist of the "tossing" phase, which requires no energy. The acceleration, of course, depends on the mass involved—a small mass can be accelerated and slowed down with little effort faster than a larger mass can. Thus we can state that within a certain margin every bone has a specific optimal speed at which energy expenditure is lowest and control is therefore highest.

For the fingers and their small mass this problem does not really exist, but it is certainly significant for the arm and the trunk. If, during a position change, the arm moves exactly parallel to the fingers, the movement will be so fast that optimal control is not possible, and the body will also be shaken. The movement of a position change will therefore have to be drawn out in time, so that the arm starts moving *before* the fingers do and the fingers execute their fast movement as the final phase. This way the mass of the arm may be accelerated more slowly since more time is available to transport it from the one position to the next.

We might compare this process with events leading to the crack of a whip. As the handle is moved back and forth relatively slowly, the tip of the whip follows this movement a little later. But the tip accelerates so much that each time the movement of the handle is reversed, the tip is pulled back with a jerk and a crack results, even though the handle itself is never jerked. In the following chapters we will be concerned with this anticipatory movement, which involves not only the arm but the entire body.

The principle of an optimal speed applies to the bow as well. If the movement is too slow it becomes hard to control; the momentum of the weight of the arm cannot be put to use. That is why a player who is nervous on stage might want to use more bow than usual to prevent the bow from trembling. The momentum of the mass will compensate for small unevennesses. If, in the opposite case, the speed of the bow becomes so great that a lot of energy is necessary to accelerate the bow or slow it down, it will be difficult to keep the same contact point on the string, and the bow will slip back and forth between the bridge and the fingerboard.

There is much greater leeway in the speed of the bow than of the left hand, for the demands for a precise goal are much higher in the case of a position change than for the bow. The bow requires greater precision of its position, but that can be checked continually, whereas the extreme precision of the position change is concentrated in an instant of time.*

Just as there exists an optimal speed (i.e., acceleration, momentum, and slowdown) for a specific movement of any part of the body, based on its mass, the coordination of the parts also has an optimal speed within a certain margin.

To use the example of the falling dominoes once more, the speed with which the movement is transmitted from piece to piece is determined by their weight and their distance from one another. To change the speed additional external force would have to be applied to each piece.

This principle applies to the body as follows: The better the movement is adjusted to the physical conditions the less energy is necessary to execute it. A position change can be executed by initiating the actual movement in the trunk or even in the right arm; analogous to that of the dominoes, this movement will be transmitted by the trunk to the left arm and hand without additional effort. The general level of muscle activity will be extremely low and the control therefore very high. If the speed is changed in either direction, extra muscle work will be necessary in every one of the involved parts either to increase or to diminish the speed.

Thus the time aspect of a compound movement shows us that looseness is based on concrete physical conditions. If a specific speed exceeds or falls short of the normal one by very much, tensions result strictly because of the physical conditions. It makes little sense to try to execute such a movement "loosely." The important consequence for cello playing is that the anticipatory

---

* This is the reason why the movement of the position change proceeds from right to left; the less-exposed right hand supports the precision of the left.

movement of a goal-directed movement, for instance, of a big shift, needs to start a certain amount of time *before* the shift, independent of the rhythmic implications of the music. For fast or even moderately fast passages, this means that the anticipatory movement might have to start several notes before the actual shift.

Since the ideal body movement is bound to physical laws, it does not necessarily follow the musical movement. Only in slow passages does the movement correspond approximately to the musical rhythm. In many cases, especially in technically difficult passages, the anticipatory movement is independent of the musical proceedings. It must start while other notes are being played, and they should not be affected by the anticipation. This procedure presupposes an important ability—in fact, the key to a virtuoso technique—namely, the ability to deal simultaneously with two time levels.

Of course, even though optimal movements obey physical laws, it does not follow that once an optimal movement is started, the continuous control of the remaining process is superfluous. After all, the aim is to achieve a continuous supersensitive control, which is possible only by keeping down the expenditure of energy.

Being conscious of all these conditions for an optimal movement is, however, only a transitory stage. The movements have to be executed completely unconsciously. If in practicing one concentrates on a specific movement process, it should only serve the purpose of coordinating it with the complete structure of the movement. Concentration means, to start with, simply isolating one part. If one does not succeed in making this part automatic by learning it thoroughly and then dismissing it from consciousness, it will threaten to break up the entire structure of the movement and instigate tightness by its very consciousness. An unconscious partial movement submits to the whole; unconscious movements are therefore looser than conscious ones. At the end of all endeavors, the musical concept alone should remain: the concept of pitch, its equivalent on the fingerboard, and the concept of sound realization with all the characteristics the bow lends to the sound.

We may now try to reformulate the law of the greatest possible economy, using the facts analysed so far:

1. A goal-directed movement has to involve the movement of as many of its joints as possible. This will avoid or at least reduce excessive acceleration and fixations of position.

2. The speed of a movement should be adapted to the conditions of the mass being moved.

3. Looseness is not primarily the cause, but rather the consequence, of a correct form of movement.

4. Changes of posture are more effective than reactive fixations for maintaining equilibrium.

5. Unconscious movements are basically more relaxed than conscious ones.

6. The first condition that must be acquired is the readiness of the involved joints to move.

Part Two

THE FINGERBOARD

IV

POSITION CHANGE

Total Body Movement during Position Change

IN STRING technique the problem of position change occupies a special place because its solution determines the ability to play in tune. It is relatively easy to remember distances within one position; even less fluent players manage to play reasonably in tune within one hand configuration. In a position change, however, the point of reference one finger has with respect to its neighbor is lost, for a big movement of the arm is necessary to reach the new tone. There is hardly any point of reference left, since, as we saw before, it is not possible to limit the movement to the forearm and keep the rest of the body motionless. Instead of trying to relate to one particular spot that might still evoke some postural memories, just as the fingers relate to one another, we have to solve the problem of position change with a harmonious movement of the entire body. Having already discussed the most important principles of such a movement, we may now look for ways to apply them to position change.

We saw earlier that a movement executed with the least effort is easiest to control. For a shift on one string we must look for the kind of movement that expends the least energy. We have encountered this kind of movement in connection with the elastic movement of the spine: If the body is turned to the left it will regain its original position without additional muscle work. If, therefore, the trunk is turned somewhat to the left shortly before an ascending shift, the energy for the position change will be made available gratis, so to speak; the arm movement will result from the elastic rebound of the spine.

We may therefore say that the equilibrium of the body is changed in such a way that the basic movement and the energy for the position change are provided when the equilibrium is restored passively. As in the case of the falling dominoes, the movement will be transmitted from this source of energy to the fingers. Little additional energy will be necessary; control of the movement will be optimal, since the only energy required is the little that corrects and controls the movement.

This procedure does not consider the bow, however. In order to include the right half of the body in the desired total movement we can go one step further.

The hand configuration required to hold the bow leaves the arm considerable freedom to move. The elbow may be very low or very high. It may move from a low position to a high one and by that movement change the equilibrium of the body in such a way that the body turns slightly to the left. If the right arm is lifted and lowered in a continuous movement—which need not affect the sound—the trunk will turn passively to the left and then to the right. Even a small turn will be sufficient for initiating a position change of the left arm. The body will not have to turn to the left actively and consciously. The impulse starts from the right arm, and its function is merged with that of the left arm into one total body motion. Thus the sound production (right arm) is coordinated in one single movement with the pitch determination (left arm).

There is one more way of initiating a passive movement of the trunk. If the speed of the bow is interrupted (and at the same time the pressure on the string is temporarily diminished), the reactive jolt will also cause a slight turning of the trunk. It is entirely possible to gain the energy for a position change from this turn, but it is more difficult to determine the exact amount of the resulting movement. In contrast to what happens when the speed is interrupted, with an experienced player lifting and lowering the arm has no effect on the sound. The arm movement may affect only the position change. Applied in practical playing, the two kinds of elastic turns can hardly be distinguished from each other.

According to this system, the descending shift will take place during the left-swing phase of such a passive turn of the trunk.

We must be aware of one thing, however: the movements described above are meaningful only if the tuning of the involved parts of the body has been achieved by training. Otherwise these recommendations will only be harmful and add meaningless movements to a body tense and inelastic from lack of use. The movement of the right arm makes sense only if the body is ready to transmit the movement from right to left.

Rotation of the Body and the Leg Muscles

We are used to considering movement as the shift of some part of the body away from or toward the trunk or as a shift of the body as a whole. In the ordinary routine of life it is not important to question what we are moving in relation to.

More careful investigation shows that we can only execute movements within the body. As mentioned before, any change in the angle of a joint by muscle contraction causes a change of position of one limb in relation to the other. The muscle contraction affects both parts of the joint in the same way. Since the acceleration of any object is dependent on its own weight as well as on the applied force, the muscle contraction on the lighter side will cause greater acceleration than that on the heavier side. If one part is prevented from moving by a firm object the entire force affects the other part.

If you flex your arm the muscle contraction affects the upper arm and the forearm equally. If someone holds your forearm, the body will move toward it; if he holds the body instead, only the forearm will move. In another example, if a pair of shears with a spring is placed on a flat surface and the two halves are allowed to snap apart, the power of the spring, which is analogous to the muscle power, will cause the angle formed by the two halves to change. Both halves will snap equally far away from their original position, in opposite directions. If one half is held firmly, the other half will snap twice as far away from its original position, i.e., the entire force will affect the movement of the one free half. If one half is weighted it will not snap as far, depending on the amount of additional weight, while the distance that the unweighted half will snap is increased by the amount the other was hindered from moving.

These examples show that a particular muscle contraction will always cause the same relative movement within the body, so that the position of the involved parts with respect to one another will change in the same way. But the absolute change of one part of the body in space is dependent on the degree to which the rest of the body is fixed.

These findings apply to position change as follows: Any movement, be it a rotation of the trunk or an arm movement, produces an energy impulse on the "stable" side that is equal and opposite to that of the visible movement. If the trunk is turned to the left, the movement takes place in relation to the pelvis and the legs; if the lower part of the body is arrested the relative movement within the body equals the absolute movement of the trunk in space. (If, instead, the trunk is arrested, the same muscle activity will cause a turn to the right of the lower suspended part of the body.) Since one does not sit on a chair with the pelvis totally fixed, every position change, every trunk rotation, in fact, shakes or shifts the very foundation of the goal-directed movement. Because of the weight of the lower part of the body and the stabilizing friction of the buttocks on the chair (and also the friction of the feet on the floor), this shift is small, but nevertheless enough to cause imprecision at the extremities, i.e., in the fingers on the fingerboard. If the foundation shifts at the moment of an important movement, the amount of energy necessary for the goal-directed movement is greater than if the base remained still.

For an ascending shift, which is accompanied by a slight rotation of the trunk to the right, the pelvis experiences a corresponding impulse to the left. (At the end of the movement it will, of course, be pulled to the right by the rotating weight of the trunk, since both parts are not completely independent in their movement.) A simple experiment will prove this: Sit straight on a chair and keep your feet under the seat. An abrupt turn of the trunk to the right will initiate a strong movement of the knees to the left. A different kind of position at the cello will diminish this big "amplitude" of the pelvis and the legs, but it will still be big enough to necessitate some corrections of the originally planned force to be exerted at the extremity, that is in the arm and hand, with the consequence of reduced precision.

To stabilize the base in relation to which the movement on the fingerboard takes place, the strong leg musculature is employed. Instead of accepting a jolt (which would be absorbed and neutralized in the lower part of the body) the base can be strengthened *before* the rotation by activating the leg musculature: for the ascending shift by using the muscles of the left leg, for the descending shift by using those of the right leg. Thus we have another total body movement, starting out in the legs and continuing all the way to the hand. The problem is as always, of course, to integrate the supporting muscle activity neatly into the total movement.

Elasticity of the Body

When we refer to a total body movement during position change we have to include yet another possible movement of the trunk. If our presupposition is correct that a fluent movement must include as many partial movements as possible, we will have to make use of the elasticity of the trunk in its forward and backward movements.

We can differentiate between two different kinds of movement:

1. The spine itself remains straight, but it is tipped forward at the pelvis.
2. The spine is curved.

This is another clear example for the necessity of coordinating the partial movements. Each of these movements, when executed separately, is unsatisfactory aesthetically. The first corresponds to a rigid and unnatural stage bow, while the second seems awkward and submissive. Only the combination of both forms of movement looks "natural." A more detailed analysis would demonstrate again that the aesthetic impression and the physical and physiological expediency coincide.

Let us apply this to position change. For the ascending shift one can bend forward slightly while turning the body and thereby give the shoulder an additional impulse, which will increase control of the movement. For the descending shift correspondingly moving backwards will be of help.

The established laws of movement also apply to the neck musculature. If the head is held in a rigid position, contractions of those muscles will affect the shoulder and limit the flexibility of the entire playing apparatus. It is therefore important that the head balance the weight shifts inherent in the playing movements. The head and the trunk are not a rigid unit—in fact, only extreme tension will make them such a unit. On the contrary they are extremely flexible in various directions.

Let us ignore for the moment the possibilities for *active* movement between the head and the trunk. We can distinguish two basically different forms of *passive* movement:

1. If the body moves forward, be it actively or as the result of an external force, the head falls back, because of the inertia of its mass. Muscle energy is necessary to avoid this movement and to pull the head forward instead. This process normally happens unconsciously, as a reflex. We can easily observe that when the body moves forward quickly, the head moves back and then catches up, so-to-speak.

2. If the head is allowed to fall forward, the body will at first move slightly backward and then forward. If the head is allowed to fall aslant to the right, the body will get an impulse to turn to the right.

In the first example the movement is initiated by the trunk, in the second by the head.

These passive movements cannot be distinguished clearly, of course; as in all body movements, active and passive phases interchange. It is important, however, that we *allow* movement, since a rigid position of the head will not permit any passive phases. Besides we have seen that any movement in a joint will raise the sensitivity threshold and therefore the precision of the goal-directed movement in space, no matter whether it is passive or active.

Since it is difficult to distinguish these movements from expressive movements of the head or body, we may assume that part of the expressive movements observed in virtuoso performers are merely their individual solutions for keeping an optimal equilibrium.

These ideas are not meant to be recipes of how and when to move the head actively or passively in which direction. Shifts and disturbances of the equilibrium are after all caused by a position change as well as by the movements of the right arm. Their complexity cannot be consciously controlled in all phases. If nothing else, a slight, harmoniously coordinated nodding and elastic swinging of the head will increase the general feeling of "relaxed" playing.

Let us emphasize once again that we are dealing with the *incorporation* of partial movements into a total body movement. Overemphasis of any such partial movement would have the same consequence as unnecessary rigidity. That explains why a simple recipe for movement does not and cannot exist. The individual differences are too great. For one player the discovery of a certain partial movement may be a stroke of genius; for another it may not mean anything since because of his particular physique he was already applying this movement.

Breathing and Position Change

In light of all the facts discussed so far, it is hardly surprising that breathing plays a decisive part in playing an optimal and precise shift. If all players breathed evenly, we might ignore this factor in this context. Even breathing, however, is interrupted not only by body movements but to a much greater extent by psychological processes. Musical circumstances play an important role here. Most string players will breathe in before they start playing, as though they had to start singing. This connection between the emotional, musical experience and its bodily equivalent is quite natural.

Psychological factors—such as fear, hope, and disappointment —influence even the technical process of playing. They have an external equivalent in the breathing, even though they are not at all or only indirectly related to the musical process. A player who is afraid of failure, even when practicing in private, will experience short breathing spasms before a difficult passage, especially before position changes. There is no physical necessity for these spasms; they are purely psychological in nature.

But while they have no physical *cause,* they certainly have clearly recognizable physical *consequences:* Breathing in quickly causes the body and especially the shoulders to shake visibly. This is another case in which, at a decisive moment when utmost control is demanded, some essential part of the body receives an uncontrollable jolt.

The movement of the hand is constantly checked by the goal conception; but when we determine and steer the energy which the finger needs to reach that goal, we cannot calculate the correction of an additional jolt. The attempt to correct at the last minute cannot be integrated harmoniously into an optimal movement drawn out in time, and instead the movement will be jerky and therefore less precise.

The precision of the shift is disturbed by the breathing spasm, just as if another person pushed the player's shoulder shortly before or during the position change. In this case the player would also unconsciously attempt a correction by adapting the amount and direction of the movement to the changed—disturbed—conditions. Any further evidence that such a movement must be less precise than an undisturbed one is superfluous.

For many players it is initially impossible to avoid such psychologically caused breathing spasms, even if their attention is alerted. A player may watch such a jolt taking place without being able to avoid it right away.

In this case an intermediate step can be recommended: When practicing hold your breath before and during the position change in order to avoid a jolt. This method cannot be a permanent solution, of course, since holding the breath does not exactly help general flexibility; but the experience of increased precision, without the jolt, can create a new sensation for the position change. If security increases, fear of failure will diminish; the jolt caused by fear will cease even when normal breathing is resumed.

Bow Direction and Position Change

The precision of the position change is influenced by yet another factor. While drawing the bow, the right arm continuously shifts the equilibrium of the body. The equilibrium is restored unconsciously either by a shift in weight or by fixating the musculature of the trunk and the legs. Therefore it makes a difference in the sensation and the physical conditions of the position change whether it occurs on the up bow or the down bow, whether it coincides with a bow change at the tip or at the frog. Thus we can differentiate between four types of ascending shifts, as shown in Fig. 1.

FIGURE 1

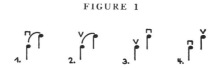

Every player knows that certain shifts are no problem on the down bow and almost always work, but are difficult to execute on the up bow.

Let us try to integrate the bowing motion of the right arm in such a way that it does not disturb the course of the movement but instead becomes the starting point of another wave of movement.

In the first type of position change shown in the diagram, we can apply the additional movement of the right arm, as mentioned above. Shortly after the elbow is lifted the body is turned to the left. When the arm is lowered again, this movement will support the swinging back of the backbone to its normal position, especially in large shifts. The down-bow movement itself tends to turn the trunk to the right, but this tendency can only be made use of at a very fast bow speed. That is why the ascending position change on a fast down bow seems to be the easiest; it automatically triggers a slight turn of the spine.

Type two is somewhat more difficult. However, if we include the passive trunk motion caused by lifting and lowering the right arm, the same result can be attained. The up bow tends to turn the trunk slightly to the left and therefore works against the desirable passive right arm. If the arm is lifted, as described above, the trunk will turn even further to the left and immediately afterwards to the right, both motions being passive. (The passive right turn may be reinforced by *lowering* the arm.) Thus, despite the up bow, a passive right turn can be used as the energy source for the position change.

Type three will initially cause a slight turn to the left, which will change into an elastic right turn during the down bow. This right turn can be made use of if the shift starts somewhat after the bow change, i.e., if an audible slide occurs on the down bow. At a slow speed the effect of the rotation is too weak, however. In this case a movement similar to types one and two may be added: The right upper arm is held higher than normal until the bow change; shortly before the bow change the elbow is lowered, resulting in a passive right turn of the trunk. This makes a smooth shift possible even at a slow bow speed.

In type four, the down bow again causes a slight turn of the trunk to the right, which can be used for the movement of the shift. The effect will be greater, though, if the right arm is lifted and then lowered before the position change and the bow change. The passive right turn thus will be postponed until the end of the down bow (when the elbow is lowered), and the turning of the spine will become clearer and rhythmically well defined.

We have already dealt with the neural interrelation of the two hands. The shift makes the left hand unsteady for a moment, and, as a consequence, the right hand often tightens, producing, in turn, negative effects in the left hand.

A fixation of the fingers of the right hand has another undesirable side effect: It forces the arm to handle the bow stroke until the very end. The natural pendulum movement of the arm during the bow change, with its gradual slowing down and gradual acceleration in the opposite direction (pp. 181–82), will be replaced by a jerky movement of the whole arm, which will cause a jolt to the body and unsteadiness in the shift.

It is perhaps unnecessary to mention again the shoulder and its role in fluent movements. In practice, however, the shoulder often proves unwilling to move, even though its flexibility is especially great. The shoulder blades and the collarbone may turn the extended arm around 90 degrees without any participation of the actual shoulder joint. The shoulder is also very flexible in the upward direction. It is an ideal compensation for any changes in equilibrium. With an inflexible shoulder, the above discussions are meaningless, since we cannot speak of fluent movement.

In general the position of the shoulder should be low; the demand for flexibility, however, is more important than this rule. In anticipation of the position change, the left shoulder may be lifted slightly within the total movement. (The right shoulder also need not stay in its low position when, for example, a fortissimo at the tip or a fast arpeggio across all four strings is required.)

Portamento and Rhythm

Another point to consider is the coordination of the two hands. A position change takes a certain amount of time, even if it is executed very quickly. We must be aware of this time, since it normally has no rhythmic value of its own. The rhythmic construction is based on the start of the tones, not on their duration. By executing the position change before the beat, even in a very slow change, we will not disturb the rhythm. The position change must be considered as a pickup; it must occur before the rhythmic stress of the new tone. If the position change takes place on one bow (as in types one and two), this fact has no special impact. The position change takes as much time from the preceding tone as it needs in order to be finished on the rhythmic stress of the new tone.

Types three and four are different in that the position change coincides with a bow change. On which part of the bow should it occur? Theoretically there are three possibilities:

1. The shift starts on the preceding bow; the bow change and the arrival on the new tone coincide with the rhythmic stress. Fig. 2 is a graphic representation of the process.

FIGURE 2

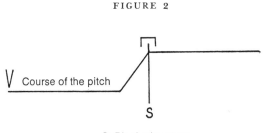

S: Rhythmic stress

2. The bow change coincides with the rhythmic stress; the shift starts on the stress and arrives at the next tone somewhat later (Fig. 3).

FIGURE 3

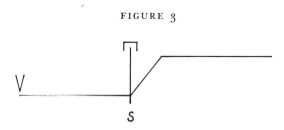

3. The shift and the bow change start before the rhythmic stress; on the rhythmic stress the new tone is reached on the already changed bow (Fig. 4).

FIGURE 4

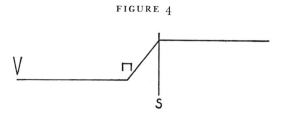

The last two possibilities are compromises because the new tone or the bow change will not coincide with the rhythmic stress. Still, the first scheme is not the best, for if the shift is audible at the end of the preceding tone it will produce an undesirable, disturbing accent. It is occasionally employed but is not satisfying aesthetically. In the second possibility, there will be no disturbing accent at the end of the preceding tone, but the next tone will be reached *after* the rhythmic stress, and the structure will become unrhythmic despite the rhythmically correct bow change. The third execution proves to be the best. The bow is changed *before* the rhythmic stress and reaches the next tone on the rhythmic stress. The shift becomes a slight pickup, which does not disturb the rhythmic structure.

Players often do not realize how long a shift takes or may not even be aware that it has a duration. They will have difficulties placing the shift *between* the down bow and the up bow unless they add a small rest, which would interrupt the flow of the phrase. The portamento of the third arrangement, however, will produce a soft "consonantal" noise* before the new tone. In practicing, the time of the shift should be lengthened in order to determine its proper position, and normally the pressure and speed of the bow would be reduced during the process. The pickup effect of the portamento can be accentuated with the bow so that the rhythmic stress is delayed even beyond the arrival at the next tone (Fig. 5). This effect, however, falls into the realm of aesthetic considerations.

FIGURE 5

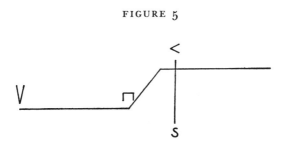

---

* *Consonantal* is used here in the phonetic sense. If we think of the musical sound produced on the cello as analogous to a vowel, then the nonmusical sound associated with the bow change can be compared to a consonant.

Movement of the Left Arm during Position Change

We have seen that the main energy for a position change need not be provided by the left arm itself. A passive right turn of the trunk, however, is not sufficient to bring about a position change. The arm must lead the hand and the fingers into the new position. In the process several kilograms of weight (1 kg = 2.2 lb) must be transported to a specific goal in a short time span.

Let us consider first the ascending position change. The arm (one may also say the elbow) is brought into its new position but the finger does not change its place on the string yet. The movement of the elbow does not describe a straight line, but a curve (Fig. 6).

FIGURE 6

Path of the Elbow in an Ascending Shift

The course of a curve of motion is determined mathematically by the initial phase of the movement. The curve of the elbow also follows such a mathematical law. Nevertheless the arm may still make corrections with respect to the envisioned goal during the first phase of the movement. The anticipatory movement determines the precision of the shift; when the actual finger movement starts there is little time for any control since the movement is too fast.

The anticipatory movement is meaningful only if it connects neatly with the final (audible) phase of the sliding motion. If the partial movements are not coordinated the actual sliding motion will have to start from a standstill again and will therefore be less controllable. During the anticipatory movement the envisioned "optical" and acoustic goal are aimed for continually. There is enough time to change the shape of the curve slightly since the movement starts rather slowly. As soon as the elbow has arrived at its new position, the forearm and hand must be pulled after it; the energy expenditure is considerably less than in the case where the whole arm participates in the final phase.

There is yet another way of reducing the energy expenditure. If the elbow is moved slightly further (lower) than its new position we may apply the principle of the double lever (which will be treated more thoroughly in connection with vibrato and string changes, see p. 192). Imagine an axis running from the shoulder to the middle of the forearm. The upper arm and part of the forearm rotate on one side of this line, the rest of the forearm and the hand on the other side. The two masses balance each other since one part of this "seesaw" uses as much energy in one direction as the other part expends in the opposite direction.

During the sliding phase of the position change this "seesaw" motion (lifting the elbow) merges with the necessary extension in the elbow joint to create a total body motion. Thus the total expenditure of energy is considerably lower and the control greater than if the forearm were merely extended from the elbow.

A slight lifting of the elbow at the end of its path causes an immediate fixation of the finger pressure on the fingerboard. Another way of saying this is that the elbow swings back elastically from its exaggerated movement into a comfortable position. If this slight lifting of the elbow is lacking, the finger will not stop at the new pitch, and additional braking energy will have to be used to keep it from sliding further. The path of the elbow is represented in Fig. 7.

FIGURE 7

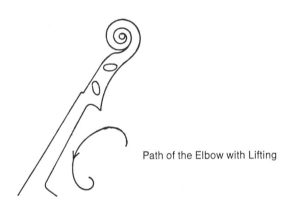

Path of the Elbow with Lifting

In its initial phase the movement of the elbow serves to lengthen the time devoted to the shift and thereby provides better control of the total movement. In its second phase the elbow movement runs perpendicular to the fingerboard and thus determines the goal; the hand and finger are pulled after it and pressed to the fingerboard in the third phase by a slight lifting of the elbow. The sliding movement of the finger starts shortly before the elbow has reached its lowest point.

This form of movement has two basic advantages:

1. The anticipatory movement prolongs the phase in which goal conception and movement may be compared and corrected.

2. The predetermined course of the curve limits possible mistakes in the end phase.

Strictly speaking, the position change therefore takes place in three phases:

1. The conceptual phase, which preceeds the others in time.

2. The anticipatory phase, which connects conception and audible execution.

3. The phase of the audible action.

It is important for precise playing that the conceptual phase indeed precede the others in time. We have to allow for the time it takes for a clear conception of the sound and the fingerboard to develop. This need for anticipation in time is not self-evident; there is a way of playing in which the player is surprised by the audible result from pitch to pitch. Success or failure, however, are determined before the audible result.

The movement for the descending shift is not simply an inversion of that of the ascending shift. For the ascending shift the arm is flung away from the body, so to speak; the anticipatory movement determines the amplitude of this flinging movement. In the descending shift the arm is pulled toward the body; one cannot fling something toward oneself. Again a movement of the trunk is involved, but the arm itself moves in a simpler curve than that of the ascending shift. A fisherman throws his fishing hook in a parabolic curve but he pulls it in in a straight line.

Nevertheless the descending shift does not consist of just a simple flexing of the elbow joint. We need not forego the advantage of transporting the moving mass to its new position before the audible movement. The elbow first moves toward the body and then pulls the hand and fingers after it. As soon as they have started moving, the elbow is lifted somewhat to increase the pressure on the arriving finger. The path of the elbow during the descending shift is represented in Fig. 8.

FIGURE 8

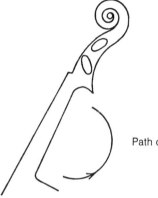

Path of the Elbow in a Descending Shift

Great acceleration requires great strength. In order to keep the level of energy low in the involved muscles, the position change should not be accelerated greatly. The acceleration of the audible part of the shift should not be too sudden either. It should be very even; this helps to coordinate the final phase into a fluent total body movement.

To avoid misunderstandings, let us repeat that it is not the *speed* of the shift that must be slow—that depends on the aesthetic requirements—but the *acceleration* of the movement that must be even, i.e., the speed will be lowest at the beginning and increase gradually from there. The moment of arrival at the new pitch means an abrupt halt for the playing finger. We have seen before, though, that this halt need not be executed as if it were in a movement parallel to the fingerboard; the arm and hand movement will aim perpendicularly at the fingerboard (to be exact, on a plane at right angles to the fingerboard) and will be intercepted by the fingerboard.

Movement of the Hand and Fingers during Position Change

The movement of the hand and fingers has to go beyond the passive movement initiated by the arm. If the forearm, hand, and fingers were a rigid unit, the precision would depend on the arm movement alone. Since the hand is a structure of many joints, keeping it still requires controlled muscle activity in order that it react appropriately to the various forces affecting it. During position change several such forces affect the hand: the pressure of the arm, which the fingers have to transfer to the string; the friction during the movement; the momentum of the arm; and gravity. It is useless to try to tense up all the hand muscles in order to create such a rigid unit artificially. The fingers are the most sensitive organs; the hand and fingers take over the fine postural nuances within the total body movement of the shift. If they were fixated an important part of the possibilities for control would be lost.

The laws of motion apply in this case as well: As many of the involved joints as possible should participate in a movement, i.e., should move within the total body movement; as few as possible should be transported along in a fixed state. As we saw before, precision *increases* this way. (In a machine precision *decreases* because of the increased number of sources of mistakes!)

For the ascending shift, the wrist and the elbow are lifted during the anticipatory movement of the arm; therefore the pressure of the finger on the string will be diminished shortly before the sliding motion begins. With a rigid wrist, the lifting of the elbow would increase the pressure, as happens at the end of a position change. It would, of course, be uneconomical to execute a position change with full finger pressure.

There is still another reason for lifting the wrist: When the elbow moves down to its new position during the anticipatory movement, the distance between it and the place where the finger makes contact gets shorter. This shortening can only be achieved by a slight flexing at the wrist (Fig. 9).

FIGURE 9

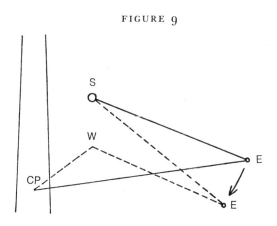

S: Shoulder, E: Elbow, W: Wrist, CP: Contact place

While the elbow is finding its new position, another angle is being changed: the forearm is supinated slightly (turned outward). And another movement is added: the wrist changes its angle not only in the dorsal-volar plane (i.e., perpendicular to the palm) but also in the plane of the palm itself by adducting the hand slightly (turning it in the direction of the thumb).

At the end of the position change the opposite actions occur: The wrist is lowered and stiffened in order to transfer the full pressure onto the string again, the forearm pronates (turns inward), and the wrist abducts (turns away from the body in the plane of the palm).

In all the finger joints minimal movements that balance the lifting and lowering of the wrist can be distinguished. The activity of the fingers, however, is not limited to those small visible movements. When the wrist and the elbow are lifted the pressure decreases, i.e., the energy expenditure of the finger muscles diminishes also since the pressure of the arm no longer needs to be supported.

When the desired pitch is arrived at this pressure increases again. At this moment, there is a possibility of making a correction at the extremities: by making small changes in the degree the fingers flex or extend when they resume the pressure. It is obvious that the fingers cannot act independently when making these corrections. The faster the pressure of the wrist increases the faster the fingers must support this pressure. Therefore the friction also increases during the last half inch, and it takes more strength to stiffen the fingers sideways against the friction. If the pressure from the wrist comes too late, the resistance of the necessary friction will be lacking and the finger will slide past the pitch. The wrist and the fingers therefore absolutely have to be supplied with sufficient pressure upon arrival at the pitch. The fingers themselves cannot exert any pressure on the string, but can only transfer that of the arm by stiffening. If you do not succeed in hitting the pitch with pressure it is by no means the fault of the fingers. If, upon arriving, the elbow swings back elastically, away from the string, the stiffening of the finger will happen as a reflex, without conscious effort (see Fig. 7). In the descending shift the action of the hand and the fingers is considerably simpler than in the ascending shift. By lowering the elbow, the finger pressure on the string is diminished. You may notice a minimal volar flexion at the wrist. The stiffening of the fingers and the wrist together with a lifting of the elbow on arrival at the pitch correspond to the movement of the ascending shift.

The mutual interdependence of all factors of the movement and its conception is dazzling. Uncertainty of conception will tempt the player to keep the pressure low when arriving at the pitch in the hope that he will still be able to make corrections. As a consequence additional muscle power is necessary to slow down the movement; and during the slowing down, the equilibrium of the body will be disturbed and the precision will suffer still more.

Even when a shift is executed correctly, a certain amount of jolting occurs upon arrival. However, it will have no negative consequences since it happens at the moment when the arm lands perpendicularly on the fingerboard—when the pitch has already been securely reached. The jolt caused by additional muscular braking action, in contrast, occurs before the pitch is reached.

It is therefore more important, when practicing, to execute the correct movement rather than to hit the correct pitch, that is, a wrong pitch arrived at in the correct way is definitely preferable to a correct pitch arrived at in the wrong way. We must accept the fact that we will make mistakes, for only by making them is the control mechanism trained. Mistakes are not failures but conditions of learning.

In order to arrive at a maximum unity of all parts, we should cultivate the conception that the hand has only one finger, namely the one pressing down the string at any given moment. This conception has its physical equivalent in the fact that the finger can be pressed down with least effort if it is an extension of the forearm axis. (This will be dealt with in greater detail in the next chapter.)

If the finger of the initial pitch is different from that of the next one, the wrist will have to take care of the switch from the original position to the following one during the shift by changing the angle of abduction (see p. 60).

The question of which finger should slide during the shift is of secondary importance in this context; the difference is more aesthetic than technical. For big shifts into the thumb position, the beginning portamento will rarely be appropriate; the end portamento (in which the exchange happens in the beginning of the shift) will be more satisfying aesthetically and more secure technically. In the lower positions we have more of a choice, especially when connecting 1–4, 1–3, 2–4. The author confesses to prefer, in general, the end portamento.

Let us now consider the function of the thumb during the shift. In the lower positions, it relaxes during the shift and may even completely leave the neck of the cello in order to keep the friction between the finger and the fingerboard as low as possible. In shifting from a lower position to the thumb, it is better to "thrust" the thumb into the higher position by pronating the forearm (after previous supination) than to slide into the position with the thumb.

The thumb has much greater flexibility than the other fingers, but it is less sensitive to how far away it is from the others. It is easier for it to be independent of the movement of the arm, and therefore it is less dependable as a sliding finger. Since we cannot do without it in this function, special training is necessary to stabilize its movement (e.g., octaves and thirds).

Finger Activity during the Anticipatory Movement

We can use one more mechanism to keep the sensitivity threshold as low as possible during the position change.

First let us perform an experiment: Hang your hand on the edge of a table by the fingertips. When you flex the fingers they will pull the hanging arm closer to the edge of the table without any effort on the part of the arm muscles. An almost identical movement can be produced if you leave the hand completely relaxed and instead actively lead the arm toward the edge of the table.

The first movement, pulling the arm by using the finger muscles, can be applied during the beginning phase of the anticipatory movement in such a way that part of the momentum of the arm (or the acceleration) is paradoxically supplied by the departing finger. The friction between the finger and the fingerboard is great enough to prevent the finger from being pulled in the direction of the arm, provided the arm is relaxed. Instead the arm will be pulled toward the contact point and will glide into the relaxed and therefore easily controlled momentum phase during the actual shift.

The ability of the strong flexing musculature of the finger to pull the arm closer therefore provides another possibility for control, even of bigger movements at the extremities of the body. The importance of this ability of the fingers, which, in contrast to the experiment on the edge of the table, also has a lateral component, applies more to the ascending than to the descending shift. But even in the latter a slight active stretch will push the arm away from the finger and therefore support the anticipatory movement, which is directed toward the nut and will, with its momentum, initiate the actual movement of the shift.

V

PLACEMENT OF FINGERS,
HAND, AND ARM
WITHIN ONE POSITION

Hand and Position

ONE OF the first terms to be introduced in string pedagogy is *position*. It is, no doubt, valuable for the beginner to organize the fingerboard conceptually, but there are two disadvantages:

1. *Position* refers to the hand rather than to the fingerboard. We are taught to imagine that the fingers are suspended exactly above the given chromatic pitches in one position, as in a machine, and need only drop vertically at the right moment.

2. In normal playing, the hand never really falls into a position; if indeed all four fingers are on the string at chromatic distances, it is only for a short time within a fast passage. When playing moderately fast, the movement of the hand has nothing in common with the idea of the position.

We will keep the term *position* for practical purposes, i.e., in order to describe the "geography" of the fingerboard. The only constants are the chromatic distances on the fingerboard itself. It is of no importance for the pitch which finger in which position presses down the string to get a certain tone on the only possible spot.

A certain minimum of pressure is required to press down the string in such a way that an unambiguous pitch results, i.e., so that the string cannot move at the contact place even when it is vibrating at a large amplitude. The necessary pressure will often be far more than one kilogram (2 lb). This means a considerable strain, especially on the 4th finger, which is the weakest. This energy requirement must be kept in mind when looking for the best position in each case.

If the hand corresponded to the typical mechanical image of the position, its function could be described in a few sentences. The four fingers would be of even strength and even length, would be placed at chromatic distances from one another, and would all have the same functions. They would be situated side by side on an axis running parallel to the neck of the cello. Only the knuckles (see footnote p. 29) would have to move; the joints on either side would not have to be considered. The axis itself would be conceived of as stationary and it would require no energy to stay in place.

Such a mechanical image, even when stated less bluntly, does not depict the real conditions of the hand. In fact, the hand seems to be especially unsuited to placing the fingers on a straight line (the string) at even distances.

1. The fingers vary in length.
2. The fingers vary in strength.
3. Their ability to spread apart is different; there is less spread between the 2nd and 3rd fingers than between the 3rd and 4th or the 1st and 2nd.
4. Since the fingers may spread apart to a greater or lesser

extent, the distance between two fingers cannot be derived from the previous configuration; it must be measured out anew every time.

5. When the knuckles are moving, the joints on either side of them have to be activated as well, in relation to the amount of pressure exerted.

6. The last joints of the flexed fingers are not parallel.

7. The fingertips vary in width.

8. The knuckles do not lie on a straight line.

Instead of trying to prescribe a mechanical scheme for the hand and thereby accept several disadvantages, it seems more sensible to examine which finger, hand, and arm positions allow for the best conditions of pressure and movement for each of the fingers.

The First Four Positions

Place the 1st finger on B on the A string. It is obvious that the finger must press perpendicularly on the fingerboard. Now put the finger down so that the last joint is perpendicular to the string. That can only be achieved by supinating the forearm considerably. The most comfortable position of a joint, however, is almost always one that is halfway between its two extreme positions. When the forearm is in an extremely pronated position the palm faces outward. In between these two extremes the most comfortable position appears to be the one in which the palm faces the ground.

Another disadvantage of the perpendicular position of the last joint is that the supination does not allow the other fingers to rise very far from the string. A fair distance is needed for the finger to strike the string smartly so that a clear articulation ("percussion") is guaranteed.

Finally, it is difficult in a supinated position to separate the 2nd and 3rd fingers sufficiently to encompass a half step. The only advantage of a supinated position is that the finger hits the string exactly in the direction of the pressure. Since it would entail three serious disadvantages, this position must be declared impractical, apart from a few exceptions that will be discussed later.

Now place the finger in a slanted position, so that the palm is approximately horizontal. The angle formed by the string and the finger will be approximately 30°–40° (see Fig. 10). The elbow

FIGURE 10

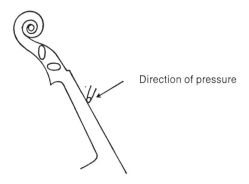

Direction of pressure

stays in its original place. In this position the disadvantages mentioned above will be avoided: The axis of the forearm has a comfortable position, the free fingers can hit the string from a sufficient distance, and the space between the 2nd and 3rd fingers can be increased by flexing the 2nd somewhat more.

But new disadvantages result: The 1st finger is forced to press partly in a lateral direction. The other fingers also hit the string in a lateral direction, which might make them slip slightly toward the bridge and therefore stop the string incorrectly (see Fig. 11).

FIGURE 11

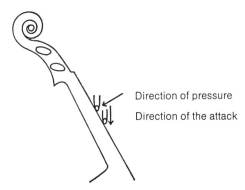

Direction of pressure

Direction of the attack

There is, however, a simple means by which both of these effects can almost be eliminated. If the elbow is moved back so that it is almost behind the body, the direction of the pressure of the 1st finger and the angle of attack of the other fingers will again approach a direction perpendicular to the fingerboard without changing the *angle* between the string and the last joint of the finger (Fig. 12).

FIGURE 12

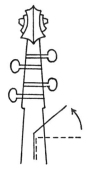

Change of Direction of the Forearm

It requires considerable imagination in three-dimensional space to understand these circumstances. The following may help: If the flexed 1st finger is placed on the string in such a way that the plane of the palm is parallel to the surface of the fingerboard and the plane of the finger is perpendicular to it, the direction of the pressure will be exactly perpendicular to the fingerboard. From the side it will look like Fig. 13. This extreme position, of

FIGURE 13

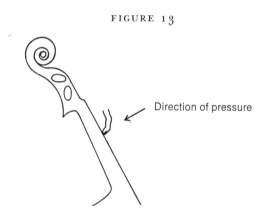

Direction of pressure

course, is not practicable. But one may keep the knuckle of the 1st finger about 5 centimeters (2 inches) closer to the nut than the contact point of the fingertip. The 2nd finger can also hit the string perpendicularly from this position. But let us remain with the 1st.

The angle formed by the finger and the string is now most advantageous for the application of force by the 1st finger. As long as the other fingers are not used they will stay close to one another and will assist the 1st finger in pressing down the string. In this position the hand is most relaxed. (It makes little sense to expect the other fingers to remain in position, suspended over their contact places.)

The thumb is located opposite the 1st finger, perhaps even a little further toward the nut. As long as the 1st finger exerts pressure, the thumb will counteract that pressure. Pressure and counterpressure correspond to the basic grasping movement of the hand. There is no reason to eliminate this natural counterpressure. Especially while vibrating, the counterpressure of the thumb has a stabilizing effect on the rotating motion of the hand. To demand a basically "relaxed" thumb would therefore be contrary to the natural disposition of the hand. (There are a few cases in which it may be more comfortable to take the thumb away from the neck, for instance, for stretches of a fourth.)

Too much importance is often attached to the flexing of the left thumb. It is quite irrelevant whether the thumb is extended or flexed. The disadvantages of a right thumb that is flexed too much (p. 157) do not apply for the left one. The thumb may be flexed or extended, relaxed or activated, according to the demands of the playing.

Now put the 2nd finger down. If we assume that a pressure of 1.5 kilograms (3 lb) is necessary to press the string to the fingerboard, the total pressure of the arm, if the pressure of the 1st finger is maintained, will now increase to 3 kilograms (6 lb). Therefore the 1st finger can relax when the 2nd is put down. This way the pressure relations in the arm do not change. It does not matter whether the 1st finger, with its own few grams, stays down lightly or whether it is lifted off the string; in general it will probably be lifted slightly.

The thumb relaxes while the fingers change, moves closer to the little finger, and is activated anew to form another "pair of pliers" with the 2nd finger. It does not come to rest right opposite the 2nd finger, however. The further it moves toward the little finger the more uncomfortable its position becomes. Therefore we must find a compromise between an uncomfortable position and the necessary counterpressure to the playing finger.

In looking for the most comfortable position the following must also be considered: If the 1st and 4th fingers are pressed alternately on a table, the hand changes its angle of abduction at the wrist. For the 1st finger it is more abducted (turned to the left), for the 4th finger more adducted (turned to the right). The arm moves into a position in which the contact point of the finger is in a continuous line with the forearm axis. If the contact point is outside the extension of this axis, certain rotating muscles must be activated in the forearm in order to counteract the resistance of the table so that the hand will not "topple over."

In the change from the 1st to the 2nd finger we can therefore observe a small change in the angle formed with the wrist: The 2nd finger now becomes the continuation of the forearm axis. This means that the hand will also pull the elbow into a different position. It moves a little toward the bridge, parallel to the neck of the cello (Fig. 14). Before the finger comes down it is flexed and

FIGURE 14

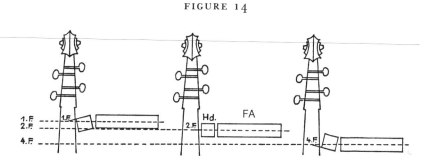

F: Finger, Hd: Hand, FA: Forearm

spread away appropriately; this adjustment forms a harmonious and continuous movement with the last phase of this total movement, which is the actual putting down of the finger.

When changing from the 2nd to the 3rd and from the 3rd to the 4th finger, the movement of the elbow becomes clearer still. Since the 3rd finger is shorter than the 2nd, and the 4th is shorter than the 3rd, the arm must make up for the difference in length— the elbow therefore moves to a still lower position. The hand is more supinated for the 4th finger than it is for the 1st, since the 4th is on the "supination side" of the forearm.

The thumb moves (of course, only when playing slowly) a little further toward the little finger when changing from the 2nd finger to the 3rd and from the 3rd to the 4th; when playing with the 4th finger the thumb will be just about opposite the 2nd finger or even a little farther toward the bridge. If the thumb moves closer to the little finger, its first joint will naturally flex more and more. It will generally be flexed more when playing with the 4th finger than when playing with the 1st. When all four fingers move fast, it becomes meaningless for the thumb to move along; it stays in a medium position, about opposite the space between the 1st and 2nd fingers. This is also the case when playing thirds or sevenths.

The difficulties in creating a big enough distance between the 2nd and 3rd fingers in the lower positions cannot be blamed on the fact that the 3rd finger cannot be spread away sufficiently. Since

FIGURE 15

both fingers are flexed at the same time any spreading is undone again; in a flexed position the last joints form an angle with each other if the fingers are spread apart considerably. In practical playing, this disadvantage can be counteracted by not putting the 2nd and 3rd fingers down at the same time, but one after the other. In playing a half step from the 2nd to the 3rd finger, the 2nd must press the string down firmly. Then the hand is pulled toward the little finger, the 2nd finger will stay in its place with pressure while the 3rd can easily be pulled into its correct position. When changing from the 3rd to the 2nd finger this process is reversed.

It is less important to determine whether the 3rd finger should be put down together with the 4th. As we saw before, it would be a waste of energy to keep the 3rd finger down with full pressure when it is not being used. However, it may stay on the string with its own weight or even a little bit more. In any case, the pressure of the 4th finger will decrease the more the 3rd continues to press, unless the arm applies additional pressure.

The previously discussed elbow motion becomes even larger in the "extended position," i.e., when the distance between the 1st and 4th fingers becomes a major third.

Thus, even within one position, a number of differentiated movements are required. Within the same position, the difference between the placement of the arm for the extended 1st finger and for the 4th is much greater than the difference in its placement when the same finger is used in two neighboring positions. The arm assumes a position in which the position of each finger is most comfortable and therefore the pressure conditions are most favorable. This, of course, applies only when the speed is moderate and when the individual fingers are put down one after another.

In very fast passages within one position, the adjusting movements of the arm would have to be so fast that the principle of the greatest possible economy of energy expenditure would be violated. Therefore the arm must take a medium position between the extreme positions of the 1st and the 4th fingers and increasingly leave the movement to the fingers. The mechanism of forearm rotation (1st finger more pronated, 4th more supinated) can, however, still be used; in most cases a small elbow movement will remain. In fast passages it is more economical to leave the lower fingers on the string since they will be in use again soon. This does not, however, mean that the pressure will stay constant; even the finger that stays on the string can temporarily release its pressure in favor of the playing finger and increase the pressure again at the moment it is playing.

For double stops of thirds or sevenths we are forced to put down all the fingers. Here again the position of the elbow will be about in the middle between the positions for the 1st and the 4th finger. For a third the elbow will be lower than for a seventh in order to support the required hand position.

FIGURE 16

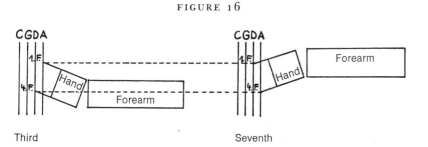

Third   Seventh

When all four fingers are on the string at the same time, the variation in their length is especially noticeable. Since the fingertips are put down on a straight line, i.e., the string, their degree of flexing will vary. The last joints of the 1st and 2nd fingers will be on a plane perpendicular to the fingerboard, the 3rd finger will be less flexed, and the 4th will be almost straight.

The hand has to be able to stretch for a whole step between the 1st and the 2nd finger. If both are flexed, simply spreading the 1st finger will not be sufficient to achieve the necessary distance. The hand must be put in a positon in which either an additional flexing or extending of the 1st finger becomes possible. If the 2nd finger is put down in a normal position so that the knuckle is above the contact place (closer to the nut), the distance of a whole step or more can easily be reached by flexing the 1st finger and simultaneously extending the 2nd. The 1st finger will also be in its best position—hitting the string diagonally from above. When the 2nd finger is extended, though, the 3rd and 4th will be pulled toward the nut also. In this position it is barely possible for the 4th finger to reach for a whole step above the 2nd (see Fig. 17a).

FIGURE 17

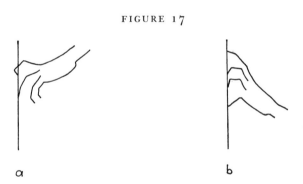

a   b

In all cases where the 4th finger is needed simultaneously with or right before or after the 1st finger, it is therefore necessary to reach for the whole step between the 1st and 2nd fingers by *extending* the 1st. If the 1st finger is extended in a normal hand position, the fingertip moves toward the next lower string, even if it is spread far away at the same time. In order to make up for this, the axis of the hand must be brought into a different angle with the string. Instead of coming from above (from the nut), the hand must come from below (in which case the forearm must also be more supinated than normal). The elbow will also assume a position closer to the bridge than in its normal position (see Fig. 17b). In this position, the 1st finger can easily reach the distance of a whole step from the 2nd, but it also ceases to be a continuation of the forearm axis, i.e., it is far from a position of the best pressure conditions.

In playing a stretch from the 4th to the 1st finger or from the 1st to the 4th, the arm and the hand will, therefore, at first assume a position in which the elbow is *low;* as soon as the 1st (or 4th) finger is put down, the elbow will move back (toward the nut) again. Only for fast movements within the hand or for thirds and sevenths, must we retain the stretch in the 1st finger and the resulting lower position of the elbow.

In vibrato the positions of the arm, the hand, and the fingers are of great importance also (see chap. 7). Let us merely mention now that a hanging elbow limits the flexibility of the entire left arm. Vibrato, flexibility of the fingers, and shifts are severely impaired by such a "lazy" position.

The observations made here in connection with the first position are analogous for the second, third, and fourth positions. The elbow will have an appropriately lower and more forward position; it changes its position parallel to the neck of the cello. In order to complete this discussion the following attendant changes of position should be listed:

1. The shoulder also moves somewhat toward the bridge, parallel to the neck of the cello.

2. At the same time the angle between the shoulder and the upper arm changes.

3. In addition to the stretch in the elbow joint, the upper arm rotates inward; if this rotation were prevented, the hand would move away from the neck of the cello.

The Transitional Positions (Fifth to Seventh)

The obtuse angle formed by the hand and the forearm does not change between the first and the fourth positions. (For the A string the angle is dorsal; that is, it is formed by the back of the hand and the forearm. For the C string it is volar; the angle is now formed by the palm by the inner side of the forearm.) It is theoretically possible to reach the fifth through seventh positions without changing this angle; however, the arm would have to be brought into an extremely high position to avoid touching the edge of the cello.

Therefore, in the transitional positions let us keep the wrist in almost the same spot it is in for the fourth position and, instead, change the angle the hand forms with the forearm in several ways:

1. The hand increasingly flexes (volarly) with each higher transitional position.

2. At the same time the hand abducts increasingly.

3. The forearm is increasingly pronated.

The more acute the angle formed by the hand and the string becomes, the less the 4th finger can be used. For the octave above the open string it may still be used; any higher than that the use of the 4th finger would entail a very uncomfortable arm position coupled with an overly flexed 2nd finger. Because of its length the 2nd finger would have to be pulled toward the string in a way that the last joint would tip over and it would become impossible to keep the fingernail from touching the fingerboard. It is therefore preferable to dispense with the 4th finger entirely and to put the by now smaller distance of the whole step between the 2nd and the 3rd finger.

The required stretch between the 1st and the 3rd finger (Fig. 18) has one disadvantage, however. In the lower positions we had

FIGURE 18

a choice between flexing and extending the 1st finger for the extended position. In the transitional positions, however, the axis
of the hand forms an acute angle with the string so that the elbow
cannot be lowered sufficiently to allow for an extension of the 1st
finger. To reach the distance of a major third the only possibility
is to flex the 1st finger extremely and extend the 3rd.

The only position in which this stretch is problematic is the
fifth; in higher positions the intervals become smaller so that the
distance becomes more comfortable again (as in Fig. 19). But even

FIGURE 19

in these positions it is advisable to maintain the extended position
of the hand only in fast passages or in double stops in which it
cannot be avoided. In slow sequences of tones it should be used
only for the short moment when changing from the 1st to the 3rd
finger and immediately abandoned in order to attain a position
more favorable for pressure and vibrato.

The position of the thumb will be partly determined by the
build of the player's hand. With a big hand, the thumb may re-

main in the curve of the neck of the cello even in the seventh position; with a small hand, the thumb moves to the side of the curve or, during a strong vibrato, leaves the neck altogether.

The purpose of the pressure of the thumb is to provide stabilization for the pressure of the playing finger. If the finger moves away from a position opposite the thumb the pressure of the thumb makes less and less sense. Therefore the higher the position the less the thumb pressure. In the seventh position any pressure of the thumb against the neck will be superfluous; it will not help the playing finger and might detract from the vibrato.

The Thumb Positions

If we presuppose that the thumb is used as a playing finger mainly in the higher positions, we can say that the axis of the hand will form a more acute angle with the string the farther the hand moves toward the bridge. That means that the 1st finger will have to be flexed strongly, the 2nd flexed normally, and the 3rd will have to be extended.

While in the lower positions intonation is mainly determined by the degree to which the fingers are spread apart, in the upper positions it becomes more and more important how much the fingers are flexed or extended. In order to use the 4th finger in the thumb positions, too, the 1st finger will have to be flexed so strongly that the fingernail will inevitably touch the string, the 2nd finger also will have to be flexed strongly, and in order to make up for the short 4th finger the arm will have to be lowered considerably and the hand brought into a position of adduction. The entire position becomes so unfavorable to playing fluently that it may be recommended only if the use of the 4th finger cannot be avoided. In that case, it is wise to take the 1st and 2nd fingers off the string to prevent their nails from touching the fingerboard. The strongly flexed 1st finger is most annoying when it is necessary to play a half step between the thumb and the 1st finger, for the nail of the 1st finger will usually touch the fingerboard.

There are several possible ways to compensate for the resulting insecure contact of the finger:

1. The last joint collapses. The fingertip, not the nail, is pressed on the string, and vibrato is guaranteed. This, however, is only possible in a moderately fast tempo since, in order to collapse against the resistance of the fingerboard, the fingers must already be resting on the fingerboard.

2. If not used within the position, the thumb may be taken off the string. The 1st finger thus may be flexed less so that the nail need not touch the string.

3. The thumb does not press the string down completely. The 1st finger is able to push the string sideways from right to left; this does not result in a brilliant sound, but the finger will not slip in fast passages.

4. The string is grasped between the nail and the flesh; in this case the string is again not pressed to the fingerboard completely, but the resulting sound is clear.

5. Hardly elegant, but in certain cases applicable as a last resort, is a strongly flexed 1st finger pressing down on the string with its nail.

6. The last possibility is to choose a different fingering. It is often much easier to change positions than to play in the same position under unfavorable circumstances.

The nature of the thumb is such that its main strength is directed toward the other fingers, with which it forms a grasping mechanism. For the thumb positions its strength has to be exerted downward, away from the palm, a direction that is by nature less developed. The thumb therefore tires faster than the other fingers.

In addition it needs to be stronger than the other fingers because it normally must press down two strings at a time.

We must examine this fact more closely. We saw before that it is not expedient to keep pressing down with a finger once the next higher one is being used for playing. This principle also applies to the thumb. Let us suppose that the thumb presses down on a string with a weight of 1 kilogram (2 lb). At the moment that a different finger is used and is pressed on the string with 1 kilogram of weight, the thumb decreases its pressure as much as possible; the higher finger now takes care of pressing the string to the fingerboard. Only when reapplied, does the thumb alone exert the full pressure. In this way the total pressure of the arm stays the same; its support goes almost exclusively to whichever finger is playing at the time. Whether the other fingers leave the string altogether or whether they stay down with their own weight does not change the principle. If the arm pressure remains the same, the pressure applied by the playing finger is reduced by the amount a lower one uses to press down the string. Conversely, the playing finger is relieved automatically of the amount of pressure exerted by a higher finger as it starts pressing on the string.

The full *double* pressure of the thumb on two strings is therefore only required for fifths. If the forearm changes its position the thumb can diminish the pressure exerted on either the upper or the lower string. If the elbow is low the pressure is only on the higher string; if it is high only the lower string is pressed down completely.

FIGURE 20

a   b

Thus we are able to realize the basic goal for the greatest possible economy in the thumb positions, by adapting the expenditure of energy to the particular circumstances. It should be emphasized once more that this demand by no means implies that the least visible motion is the most economical. In contrast to a machine for which exterior calmness means inactivity, each position of our body requires uninterrupted muscle activity. An uncomfortable position, therefore, violates this demand even before there is any movement. If one succeeds in reaching a more favorable position from a position that is wasting energy, a large movement is more economical than staying in the original position.

String Crossings and Double Stops

For the low strings the elbow is held somewhat higher than for the high strings. Using the neck of the cello as an axis, the forearm turns around it in order to reach the lower strings. If the arm alone were to make a change of position for the lower strings, the difference between its position for the A string and for the C string would be very large. The elbow would be in such a high position for the C string that a disproportionate amount of energy would be required to hold up the shoulder and the arm. For this reason, the hand changes the angle it forms with the forearm for the lower strings. The angle is slightly dorsal for the A string, but the hand is flexed somewhat volarly for the C string. The wrist thus is higher for the low strings than for the high ones.

For fast string crossings, the individual finger will be flexed or extended, whichever is needed to round off the movement: a more flexed finger position on the high strings and a more extended one on the low ones. It would require too abrupt an arm movement if the finger were to be kept flexed in a specific way.

With double stops and chords also we can observe that the

fingers are flexed to a different degree on the different strings. The arm follows the requirements of the string as well as those of the fingers.

Since each string requires a minimum pressure to press it down firmly, and since in a chord the pressure necessary to press down all the strings is added together, the arm cannot manage a four-string chord with its own weight. Either the counterpressure of the thumb must increase or the arm must press down actively. If each string bears 1 kilogram of pressure, a four-string chord requires a total of 4 kilograms.

Let us sum up the most important results of our discussion of the position of the fingers, the hand, and the arm:

1. The first demand is for the greatest possible economy of the expenditure of energy.

2. We thus have to look for the most comfortable position for each purpose.

3. The size of a movement does not allow any inference about the economy of the energy expenditure.

4. For each playing finger there is a specific, optimal position of the hand and the arm.

5. For each string there is an optimal position of the hand and the arm.

6. For each place on the fingerboard there is an optimal position of the hand and the arm.

7. The pressure needed to push the string down firmly is at least 1 kilogram. For double stops and chords the pressures on each individual string added together equal the total pressure of the arm.

8. The angle formed by the axis of the hand and the string becomes more acute the higher the position and requires a considerable change in the degree the fingers are flexed.

9. In the lower positions the pressure of the thumb, combined with that of the other fingers, works like a "pair of pliers"; when changing fingers (and positions) the thumb relaxes momentarily. In the transitional positions the pressure of the thumb loses its function and is therefore diminished.

10. For the A string, the wrist is held in a dorsal position; for the C string it is flexed slightly volarly.

In fluent playing, the entire left arm is continually in motion in order to support the changing action of the fingers. There is no one basic position for the arm. At most it might be justified when teaching a beginner to ask for such a position as a point of departure.

VI

MOVEMENT
WITHIN THE HAND

Percussion

WE HAVE mentioned before that a certain minimum energy is necessary to press the vibrating string firmly against the fingerboard. This minimum energy is related to the volume. Each individual vibration creates an energy impulse in the direction of the swinging mass of the string. The string "pushes the finger away" with each vibration. Since this resistance is greater the larger the amplitude, to stop the string completely the finger must press harder for loud sounds than for soft ones, and when changing pitches, the *speed* with which the new finger hits the string must also be greater for loud playing than for soft.

The fact that the amplitude increases toward the middle of the string must also be considered. In changing to a higher pitch on the same string, if the new finger is put down close to the previous one, the amplitude of the new contact place will be smaller than if the finger is put down farther away. Just as the amplitude is larger for the bow at the fingerboard than at the bridge, the amplitude for the left hand is larger the bigger the distance between two successive fingers when changing to a higher pitch on the same string.

An immediate cutoff of any point of a string vibrating at a large amplitude requires greater energy than a cutoff at a small amplitude. We may therefore say that it takes less strength to press down a string at a small interval from the previous pitch and make it respond properly than it takes for a larger interval.

All these reflections lead us to the term *percussion,* which Pablo Casals introduced into cello technique. The basis of this term is the aesthetic consideration that expressive playing requires that the beginning of a pitch must be clear and sure. *Percussion* therefore is a strong articulation with the finger. In addition to the clear separation of the two pitches, it results in a slight "plosive" noise* when the fingerboard is hit. This noise must melt into the actual attack of the sound, for it is not desirable to hear the finger hit the fingerboard.

In any case, the finger muscles must be strengthened. There is no way around that. Nevertheless, during the actual playing, all possible help must be given to facilitate the work of the fingers. One simple reflection in this connection: the impact of the finger hitting the string depends on the mass of the finger and the speed with which it meets the fingerboard. The mass is constant and we may ignore it by saying that the impact of hitting the string is proportionate to the speed with which the finger meets the fingerboard. This speed, in turn, is dependent on the available strength and the distance involved.

Let us suppose that the available strength of the finger stays constant. Then the finger will meet the fingerboard with greater speed (percussion) the larger the distance is, since the finger accelerates evenly during the entire distance. But the fingers are not of

* The phonetic term *plosive,* as in the consonant *p,* best describes this sound.

even strength. The strong 2nd finger will need a shorter distance for a clear percussion than will the weak 4th finger. As a rule, the distance will normally be longer for the 4th finger than for the 2nd.

The hand position in which the palm is horizontal (and not parallel to the fingerboard) is of great advantage in this respect. The distance to the fingerboard becomes larger for each successive finger; for the 4th finger it is the largest (see Fig. 21).

FIGURE 21

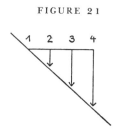

Shortly before the finger comes down (flexes at the knuckle), the two last joints are extended slightly so that the finger may hit the string perpendicularly. When the finger is lifted off the string (extension of the knuckle), as in a descending passage, there is also a slight flexion of the middle joint of the finger. This means that, with the exception of trills, putting the finger down is not the exact reversal of lifting it.

The simultaneous flexion of the middle and last joints when the finger is lifted off has one advantage (see Fig. 22). Just as percussion helps to fix the beginning of the pitch clearly when the finger is put down, a slight pizzicato occurs when it is lifted off and simultaneously flexed. This produces a clear beginning of the pitch in a descending line. This plucking, however, is not as essential for a clear change as the percussion is for the ascending line. When the higher finger is lifted off, the lower one is already

FIGURE 22

keeping the string down at a point where it is not vibrating. Nevertheless the finger must be lifted off the string quickly so that no artificial harmonic is produced at the moment when one finger is pressing the string down hard and the other is pressing it lightly. By plucking, this demand is fulfilled, for the finger leaves the string suddenly.

It is, by the way, legitimate to use the rotating mechanism of the forearm (in the supinated direction) to support the percussion of the 4th finger. A natural movement is normally composed of several individual movements, as we saw before. We have to learn how to isolate certain movements to be sure that no disturbing unconscious reflexes accompany the movement; if such accompanying movements have a supporting function, however, as in the example of the 4th finger and the supination, there is no reason to reject such help.

For pedagogic reasons it is important to develop the percussion function in each individual finger as far as possible without such help. Let us remember that the degree of percussion is not only proportionate to the strength but also to the distance. If the finger comes down on the string from a greater distance, it *seems* stronger than a stronger finger that comes down from a smaller distance. For this reason it might be useful to raise the finger higher than its natural position right before it comes down in order to achieve a clear percussion—we "cock" the finger back as we do the arm before throwing a ball.

We may describe the action of one finger being put down and then lifted off the string (for example, the change from the 1st to the 4th to the 1st finger) in slow motion as follows:

1. The 4th finger is held in a position that is most comfortable for the preceding 1st finger, but not above its own contact place.

2. The 4th finger approaches the point above its contact place and at the same time is cocked back.

3. The arm supports this movement and approaches the position that is most comfortable for the next tone; the elbow moves toward the bridge, parallel to the fingerboard.

4. Now the 4th finger hits the string, supported by supination.

5. The arm adjusts to the position of the finger (the contact point becomes the continuation of the forearm axis).

6. The pressure of the 1st finger decreases; it may leave the string; the pressure is on the 4th finger.

7. In the reverse procedure, the 1st finger assumes its position on the string without percussion; the elbow is moved back properly.

8. The knuckle of the 4th finger is extended and the last joints are flexed, resulting in a slight plucking of the string.

9. At this moment the entire pressure of the arm is transferred to the 1st finger, which in turn stiffens.

10. The arm moves to the position that is most appropriate for the 1st finger.

We see now that the actual movement of the finger is considerably different from the mechanical image on which a machine constructed to shorten the string would be based. The mechanical "finger" would always have to stay above the contact place; one single impulse would let it fall or lift it off. There would be no adjustment necessary in the fingers, the hand, or the arm.

The Trill

The execution of a trill, however, comes closer to the mechanical model. When the same finger is put down and lifted off in rapid succession, there is not sufficient time to adjust to a different position. In this one case, therefore, the finger must be suspended exactly above the contact place.

It would, of course, be a simplification to describe the trill as a movement solely of the knuckle. Theoretically there are four ways of producing a trill on the cello:

1. By using the knuckle.
2. By using the wrist.
3. By rotation of the forearm.
4. By vibrato of the upper arm.

In actual playing, we generally use a combination of these forms. Let us examine these possibilities more closely.

1. The trill that is executed solely by the knuckle is limited in speed. We can show that with a simple experiment: Place the left hand flat on a table and knock rhythmically on the table with each individual finger as fast as possible, keeping the fingers that are not trilling on the table. A distance of at least 2 centimeters (1 inch) is needed for a minimum percussion. By this method not even well-trained fingers can come close to the speed necessary for a virtuoso trill. Even at a slow speed it is difficult to keep the rhythm and the strength of the percussion constant. The speed of the trill may be increased by reducing the distance from the table to a few millimeters, but for an actual trill on a string this distance would be too short to guarantee a clear separation of pitch. We must therefore abandon the idea that the trill can be created by the knuckle alone. If the other fingers are allowed to

leave the table, the trill will improve considerably; this adds a small wrist movement, hardly noticeable, but effective.

2. Now also lift the palm from the table and try to trill as fast as possible from a distance of about 2 centimeters. It is possible to trill much faster than it was with knuckle action alone. The reason is a quite distinct movement in the wrist in a dorsal-volar direction. The stationary finger is elastic enough to absorb this movement, while the trilling finger can use a movement combining wrist and knuckle action at fast speed, working from a sufficient distance. Experimentally it is also possible to dispense with the knuckle action and to transfer the entire movement to the wrist. Occasionally this might be applied to relieve the knuckle function temporarily. The volar-dorsal movement of the wrist is one of the fastest active repetitive movements the body has at its disposal. Individual differences can, of course, be noticed, but it will help a virtuoso trill in any case to involve the wrist.

These experiments show that the result does not always depend on the strength within one isolated movement; often a proper combination of several movements is considerably more effective than one well-developed movement that is not coordinated with the others.

3. The wrist trill leads us to one that is created by rotating the forearm. If the trilling finger is kept close to the string and the forearm rotates quickly back and forth, a very fast trill will result, again without any knuckle action. This trill is created by the same "motor" as the vibrato of the forearm (see chap. 7). Close observation is necessary, however, to distinguish this action from a passive forearm rotation that results when the hand leans on the stationary finger and the wrist is moved up and down actively. In practice, both forms will be combined. The original movement of the finger trilling from the knuckle is doubly reinforced now: by the wrist and by the forearm rotation. Fast and clearly articulated trills can be achieved in this fashion; exhaustion in a long series of

trills can be avoided by alternately stressing wrist movement and forearm rotation.

4. The function of upper arm rotation will be discussed in detail in the next chapter. Let us mention now that the trill may also be executed with the normal vibrato of the upper arm. In this "vibrato trill" the rotating motion is transformed into an up-and-down motion of the trilling finger, as in the active forearm rotation. Again the other partial movements (rotation of the forearm, movement of the wrist and of the knuckles) may be integrated into the process, giving us a strong, fast trill that can be kept up for long stretches.

Even though each of the partial functions must be developed and strengthened by itself, it would be absurd to ban any of them from the technique altogether. (One hears occasionally that using the vibrato mechanism for the trill is "prohibited.") Again we are dealing with differences in individual players' constitutions and preferences. The technical context may also determine the choice of the trill.

In our discussion of percussion we mentioned that the finger extends at the knuckle and flexes in the other two joints when it is lifted off the string. A fast trill with the functions of the hand and the arm described above will hardly permit any such movements; the only remaining *finger* movement is that of the knuckle. The finger is slightly flexed in the last two joints and keeps the same degree of flexion throughout the entire trill. This means that the finger is somewhat flatter during a trill than during normal vibrato playing.

Fluency

Fast-moving figures within one position present conditions similar to those of the trill. Again the fingers are generally flatter than they are during intensive vibrato playing, so that the movement of the finger is limited to the knuckle. However, there is no reason to dispense with the supporting functions of the wrist and of forearm rotation. This requires that the whole arm is always ready for movement, even if the supporting motions are only very small.

We have seen before that a fast movement is not just a slow movement speeded up but is basically a different kind of movement. In slow playing the arm assumes an optimal position for each individual tone; in fast playing, such adaptations for each finger waste energy. The hand and the arm, therefore, stay in a medium position and support the fingers only to the extent that is possible without excessive effort. A movie of slow movement shown at a fast speed will appear jerky and unnatural; fast movement at a slow speed will look tired and lame. We therefore have to examine the term *speed,* as it applies to technique, more closely.

Speed in playing differs considerably from the physical speed that is so prominent in certain sports. This aspect of sports does have an important function in instrumental technique, but we have to concede that our instrument never requires the kind of speed for any movement of the body that could not be achieved by a normal, untrained person. In instrumental technique, the term *speed* stands for the degree of coordination of several movements, none of which individually require an extremely high speed even in fast passages. *Speed,* or *fluency,* refers to the level of precision with which muscle functions of different time (rhythm) and space (e.g., intonation) can be coordinated. This speed depends very little on the actual performance strength (acceleration energy) of the muscles; if we assume that an advanced player's muscles are kept trained to a certain degree, speed, i.e., fluency, depends on the clarity of the spatial and temporal conception and on the degree of motor coordination. The temporal clarity may be achieved by sticking closely to the rhythm, once chosen; the spatial clarity has already been discussed.

It is important to know that the temporal and spatial precision influence each other: Rhythmic precision, i.e., an unambiguous conception of the starting time of the tone, reinforces spatial conception. Only then is it possible to have an overall movement pattern that proceeds harmoniously and under optimal conditions for the particular passage. A vague conception of the rhythmic process requires new "decisions" from tone to tone and therefore prevents the formation of a total movement encompassing a whole passage. Only with strict discipline, which can and should become pedantic while practicing difficult passages, can a spatial movement pattern develop that will coordinate the necessary anticipatory movements several tones beforehand.

The goal of keeping strict rhythm is not *musical* evenness in this case (even though this evenness is, of course, a by-product), but a temporal determination of each individual movement impulse ahead of time. By keeping an invariable rhythmic movement pattern, the "decision" for the movement for each individual tone becomes compulsive and therefore does not have to be made separately for each tone. The definite overall *temporal* (rhythmic-conceptual) pattern transfers its untiy to another overall pattern, the spatial one. It is the inclusion of the anticipatory movements in the total movement that makes the difficulties finally disappear; of course, this demands great mobility of the playing apparatus for virtuoso playing.

Let us summarize:

1. The degree of percussion depends on the strength of the finger and the distance to the string. A strong sound requires more percussion than a weak one.

2. In descending lines a slight plucking of the string when the finger is lifted off replaces percussion (Casals).

3. The unskilled player relies on a few basic positions and is

forced into unavoidable position changes from tone to tone. The virtuoso plans for the most comfortable positions for each passage and integrates them into an overall total motion in order to "be there" before the finger actually plays the next tone. Through ignorance the inexperienced player forgoes possible relief, i.e., he creates difficulties for himself that he then has to fight—in vain. The playing of a professional not only *looks* easier than that of an amateur; it *is*, in fact, easier.

4. There is no reason to dispense with possible support by the arm in the trill either, i.e., wrist movement and rotation of the forearm and the upper arm.

5. Movement during a fast passage looks basically different from that of a slow passage. Since in a fast passage there is no time for individual adjustments of the arm to each tone, the arm performs general movements that may include several tones.

VII

VIBRATO

Vibrato as a Means of Expression: Frequency and Amplitude

WE HAVE grown so used to vibrato on string instruments that we generally regard it as an aesthetic necessity. When asked to explain the reasons, we usually refer to the "natural" vibrato of the human voice, which is copied by the "singing" instrument. This reasoning does not, however, explain why the vibrato of the human voice is considered beautiful. Besides, simple experiments with voices that are not trained contradict the statement that vibrato is natural to the voice. Considering the strange effect of the sound of a boys' choir, which is completely without vibrato, we have to draw the conclusion that vibrato is a consciously employed means of intensifying expression.

Since vibrato is produced by a cyclic variation of the pitch (occasionally also a cyclic variation of the volume), it seems to contradict the general aim of precise intonation. Its use can be explained, however, by reference to the psychological phenomenon that one's attention is attracted more by changes in the environment than by a particular state of things.

Strictly speaking, any sound wave presents a continuous change, but its uniform course is perceived as static. Awareness of a tone is strongest at its beginning and diminishes gradually; very

97

long (and not penetratingly loud) sounds may at some point cease to be perceived at all. The continuous noises produced by a furnace or a refrigerator or the humming of a machine attract the attention only when they suddenly stop. In order to prevent a sustained tone from being noticed only at the beginning, we make cyclic changes that keep attention from declining—thus the tone will be experienced for its full duration.

Completely regular cyclic changes again become static in effect—the vibrato of an electric organ is less lively than that of a violin. Even if it were possible to change the vibrato at regular intervals, that is, accelerate it or slow it down, the regular change would soon be experienced as static.

Even for string players, this danger exists to a certain degree. In order to catch the full attention of the listener it is necessary to modify continuously a technically perfect vibrato. This fact is of particular importance because a vibrato that requires considerable exertion, as, for instance, a wide and fast vibrato does, gives the player a feeling of intensity that does not necessarily communicate itself to the listener as a musical tension.

Let us try to "condense" a tone in progress. There are three possibilities, if we disregard the dynamics of the bow:

1. The tone is started with a slowly swinging, wide vibrato; the frequency of the vibrato increases.

2. The entire tone is played with the same frequency of vibrato; the amplitude of the hand increases.

3. The tone starts with a narrow and slow amplitude; frequency and amplitude increase.

Without doubt, the third possibility effects the biggest increase in intensity, even though the total energy necessary to produce such a sound is the lowest.

The principle of attracting attention by changes may also have negative implications. If the vibrato swings irregularly, certain tiny unintentional accents develop, which disturb the musical process by superimposing themselves on the actual structure and thereby neutralizing the expression. Those small irregularities will not be perceived as such by the listener, but the structure of the phrase will not be convincing since no continuity and therefore no increase in intensity can be achieved. Hardly anybody will relate this perception to technical deficiency; it will be explained as a lack of intensity of expression on the player's part.

Vibrato Movement of the Arm

It is therefore necessary to be able to vibrate evenly. Let us start with the instrument: The cyclic variation of a pitch is created by rolling the finger back and forth on the string. The softness and elasticity of the fingertip may also vary the pitch, but since this particular movement within the flesh of the fingertip is always passive and generally follows as a side effect of the rotation, we can ignore it for the time being.

Now let us look for movements that will enable the finger to roll back and forth on the string in an absolutely regular motion. The wave of the vibrato should not only have a regular frequency; it should approach a pure sine wave (Fig. 23a), i.e., it should take the course of a pendulum. A saw-like wave (Fig. 23b) makes a nervous and jerky impression.

FIGURE 23

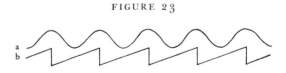

Let us explain all the possible movements that lead to such a rolling vibrato.

1. We can imagine an isolated finger movement, as is possible on the violin. The slanted finger may make the hand vibrate passively by increasing and decreasing the pressure on the string cyclically. Every time the finger increases the pressure, the hand and the arm, which are completely relaxed, are pushed a little toward the nut. This movement may be transformed into an evenly vibrating sequence in which the weight of the hand serves as a stabilizer. The pressure of the finger is great enough to prevent it from slipping off. Therefore, by merely vibrating back and forth, the hand would induce the forearm to rotate passively. The flexing muscles of the finger are the motor for this movement.

2. The movement will look almost the same when the motor is shifted to the dorsal-volar flexing muscles of the wrist. Because of the slanted position of the finger, the forearm is supinated passively by the volar flexing activity of the wrist. If the frictional resistance of the string and the fingerboard were nonexistent such a volar flexion would make the hand and the finger slide toward the bridge. The blocking, frictional resistance transforms the volar flexion into this passive supination. The hand, which wants to move toward the bridge, is forced to rotate around the axis formed by the contact place of the finger and the elbow. We have encountered similar circumstances with the trill, where a resistance transforms one movement into a different one.

3. Visually, the most obvious kind of vibrato is that of an active forearm rotation: pronation makes the finger roll toward the nut, supination toward the bridge. The big disadvantage of this kind of vibrato is that the rotation takes place around the forearm axis; outside this axis, there is almost no weight that can be used as a stabilizing pendulum. Thus, this kind of vibrato is generally fast, but it can hardly be made regular since the *entire* movement (not only its beginning) must be executed by muscle activity. In a pendulum, on the other hand (e.g., when a hanging arm is set in motion as a pendulum), the movement impulse needs

to be given only at the beginning of the vibration; the rest of the movement progresses according to physical laws with no further muscle activity.

4. Such a pendulum movement, the double leverage of the bent arm, is possible on the cello. (Details will be explained later, in connection with string change.) Since in this case the larger part of the mass is outside the rotating axis, the physical laws of mass inertia contribute to a regular course of the movement. The muscles need not control the entire movement; they only have to regulate the start.

Such a double-lever movement is created if one shakes a match box up and down to find out whether there are any matches left. The arm is bent, but the wrist has to be kept rigid so that the shaking movement will extend all the way to the hand. The elbow moves in the opposite direction to the hand. This means that there is a point on the forearm, about 6 centimeters (3 inches) below the elbow, that does not move. Imagine an axis running from that point to the shoulder. On one side of the line, the upper arm and the remaining part of the forearm rotate, and on the other side the forearm and hand rotate. This movement does not run exactly parallel to the fingerboard, but at a small acute angle to it. The main direction of the hand in any case is more or less parallel to the fingerboard.

If the finger is now placed firmly on the string, with counterpressure by the thumb, we have another passive movement similar to the wrist vibrato of number 2. The frictional resistance prevents the hand from continuing the up-and-down movement of the upper arm. Since the rotating muscles of the forearm do not give active resistance, the hand again "topples over" the contact point of the finger so that the forearm is rotated passively. As a side effect we can observe a passive flexion and extension at the elbow.

This mechanism is quite surprising because the visual result does not indicate the actual forces at work:

a. The elbow moves up and down without any participation of the flexing or lifting muscles of the arm (except in their steadying function).

b. The forearm is rotated strongly without any of the ordinarily responsible muscles contributing actively.

c. The forearm flexes and extends at the elbow without the responsible muscles moving. This lack of muscle activity may be checked easily by feeling with the right hand. Even in a wide vibrato the flexor and extensor of the forearm will not show up. But if the arm is taken away from the neck of the cello and flexed and extended alternately, an *active* movement of the forearm is called for, although it looks almost like the previous, *passive* one. Though this active flexing and extending movement may be very small, the alternate contraction (thickening) of the muscles may be clearly felt in the upper arm.

d. Rotation of the upper arm can be observed, but it is much less obvious than the other secondary, passive movement.

e. The fingers, seemingly moving the most, have no movement of their own, either active or passive, in their relation to the hand. They are, of course, kept in position by activated muscles.

f. The wrist does not show any movement of its own in relation to the forearm either. The finger and the hand must be innervated considerably to maintain their configuration. Thus, except for the rotation of the upper arm, only those joints that do not move are activated, while the moving ones (elbow and forearm rotation) are not activated.

This upper arm vibrato has one big advantage, which has been mentioned before: The mass of the arm rotates around an axis *outside* the upper arm itself; the swinging mass of the double lever requires only a short initial impulse; the rest follows the laws of inertia and of the pendulum. A large mass is disturbed less easily than a small one. (An expensive record player will have a

FIGURE 24

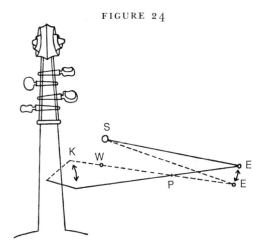

S: Shoulder, E: Elbow, P: Pivot point, W: Wrist, K: Knuckle

turntable that weighs several kilograms so that the mass overrides any possible fluctuations in the motor.)

5. Theoretically we can also produce a vibrato by flexing and extending the elbow. But since the entire mass of the forearm must be put into vibration and must be stopped twice for one double swing, the energy exerted is out of proportion to the effect of the movement, and since the arm soon tightens, this kind of vibrato cannot be recommended.

Of the five possibilities for vibrato we can also dispense with the first. The movement initiated by the finger is normally too small to be of use on the cello; another disturbing factor is that the alternate increase and decrease of the finger pressure (corresponding to the flexing of the finger) has a strong component of movement away from and toward the string. The second kind of vibrato, using primarily wrist motion, can be useful on occasion;

the amplitude can be fairly wide, and the frequency can be increased to whatever is aesthetically desirable. Especially in the upper positions, where smaller amplitude and higher frequency are required, this kind of vibrato is helpful. The third type, vibrato using only forearm rotation, seems to be subject to individual differences. It can surely be trained to be sufficiently even; its disadvantage is that the entire course of the process must be controlled actively. The frequency is somewhat greater than that of the upper arm vibrato, since the swinging mass is close to the rotating axis. (An ice skater can accelerate a spin by drawing the entire mass of the body close to the rotating axis—by pulling the arms and the free leg toward the body. If both arms are extended again the speed will diminish suddenly.)

The vibrato actually used on the cello is therefore type four. Its natural frequency is lower than those of the others; thus the player can vibrate without effort, even with a large amplitude. The vibrato tends to settle on its natural frequency, according to the kind used and the swinging mass involved. If this natural frequency is exceeded the player needs additional energy; if the frequency is not reached the swinging process becomes noticeably more difficult because it then changes into a movement that is continually controlled by the muscles. The sensation of the movement will have changed altogether.

Since the motor of the upper arm vibrato is far away from the fingers we can easily avoid certain difficulties that often hinder vibrato. Some cellists do not succeed in keeping the vibrato going while changing fingers. It is interrupted at the end of each tone and resumed after the change has taken place. Here again technical failure has its musical consequences. If the vibrato stops, the color of each tone will be changed without any musical justification, and often the result is an interruption of the musical flow of the phrase. With the big upper arm vibrato there is no active movement in the fingers, the wrist, the forearm, or the elbow joint.

The farther away from the finger the motor of the movement is the easier it becomes to separate the finger movement from it. The rhythm of the vibrato is not disturbed by the descent of the finger when the pendulum movement of the upper arm is being used, but when the vibrato is produced by active forearm rotation, it is almost impossible to make the finger hit the string during the pronation phase of the movement, and the rhythm of the vibrato is therefore destroyed.

Application of Vibrato

The frictional resistance between the finger and the fingerboard is a decisive factor for all the different kinds of vibrato. This resistance transforms the arm impulse, which is parallel to the fingerboard, into a passive rotation of the forearm. The stronger the arm impulse, i.e., the wider the vibrato, the greater the pressure of the finger must be in order to match the parallel movement of the arm and transform it into a rotation of the forearm. If the pressure is too weak, the finger will be brushed away by the movement of the arm and the hand and will slide back and forth on the fingerboard. For this reason, the pressure of the finger must sometimes considerably exceed the amount required merely to press the string to the fingerboard.

A vibrato of large amplitude is usually associated with a loud sound, a small one with a soft sound. This way both requirements, strong pressure for a large amplitude of the string and strong resistance of the finger for a wide vibrato, usually coincide. But that is not always the case.

As we saw when we examined finger movement, strong finger pressure is achieved either by great vertical pressure of the arm (weight of the arm) or by counterpressure of the thumb to the particular finger. If, in a strong vibrato, the thumb stays completely relaxed, the pressure has to be supplied by the arm alone. This does not present a strain since the weight of the arm can normally provide the necessary pressure. The firmness of the finger and therefore of its rotation axis improve considerably, however, if the thumb exerts counterpressure to the finger involved. Without that counterpressure the finger, because of its elasticity, will yield more easily to the swinging movement of the arm. If the thumb participates it will limit the elasticity of the finger and thus force the forearm to rotate passively. As mentioned before, the thumb follows the contact place of the individual finger to the extent possible without flexing the thumb excessively, since that would require additional muscle engagement.

From chapter 5 we know that in slow playing the playing finger must take its position in the continuation of the forearm axis through a change in the angle of adduction in the wrist. If the finger is not vibrated on this axis, considerably more effort is necessary to achieve the same rotating effect on the string than if the vibration takes place around this axis.

If the finger does not occupy a place on this axis, the circle that the hand describes has to be much wider. The passively vibrating mass of the forearm would be so far outside the rotating axis running from the fingertip to the elbow that the natural frequency of the vibrato would be too slow. In addition, the passive rotating effect of the forearm would be impeded. An overly strong forearm movement would take place, which would circle around the contact place with extension and flexion at the elbow.

Another individual factor is the breadth of the fingertip. It is obvious that a broad finger uses more of the string during a rotation than a narrow one. (A big wheel covers more distance in one rotation than a small one does.) Therefore the amplitude of the vibrato need not be as wide for a broad finger as for a narrow one, and for any hand the 4th finger needs a bigger vibrato movement than the 2nd does for a particular amplitude. When an intensive vibrato of wide amplitude using the 4th finger is needed, it is possible to pull and push the fingertip on its elastic flesh without any rotating movement of the finger. If the amplitude is still not wide enough, one can even go beyond the limits of this movement and allow the finger to shift its position slightly on the string.

This last variation, even if it is unorthodox, can be used successfully when a rotation of the finger is barely possible—for thirds and sevenths. Since the hand is arrested at two points, little leeway remains for a passive rotation of the forearm. The fingers will still follow the arm movement somewhat, but such a minimal rotation is not sufficient for an intensive vibrato in the lower positions. If one wishes to achieve a strong vibrato despite the restricting double position of the fingers, and attempts to produce it by sliding the fingers, it is better to relax the pressure of the thumb. The thumb is supposed to stabilize the rotational axis but if that axis hardly exists or is gone entirely, it is better for the thumb to give way to a minimal sliding on the string without any pressure on its part.

Another way to support the weak 4th finger is to combine the big upper arm vibrato with the wrist vibrato (type 2). The wrist can augment the amplitude of the upper arm vibrato so that it becomes wide enough for an intensive vibrato of the 4th finger. In extreme cases, though, one may have to resort to the sliding motion for expressive passages. The coordination of the upper arm rotation and the wrist movement is not difficult, since any wrist movement is naturally the continuation of the upper arm movement. (If the wrist is relaxed, any arm movement, including the double lever movement, will toss the hand back and forth.)

These ways of employing vibrato show up another weakness of vibrato produced by forearm rotation. Since it employs an *active* rotation, the impulse parallel to the fingerboard is lacking, making it impossible to resort to the sliding motion of the fingertip.

Vibrato and Pitch Level

There is a basic difference between the vibrato of a wind player and that of a string player. The former produces vibrato mainly by changing the *volume* of the tone—a change that also entails a slight variation in pitch. For the string player it is exactly the reverse: The vibrato is created by changing the *pitch*. An oscillograph will show, however, that the volume also changes slightly in the process. This is caused by the tiny vibrating movements of the whole instrument, which create corresponding variations in the pressure of the bow.

In an intense vibrato, the difference in pitch may be considerable, amounting to a quarter tone or more between the extremes of the amplitude. The ear still perceives a definite pitch, however, just as in a nonvibrated tone. Faulty intonation is registered even in extensively vibrated tones; deviations from the true pitch, even those that are much smaller than the amplitude of the vibrato itself, are still clearly distinguished. It is therefore not true that, in a wide vibrato, the listener is free to select any pitches between the two extremes. Why is that?

From an evenly vibrating tone the ear chooses a medium frequency as the main pitch impression. Thus, the tone that the listener hears is exactly in the middle between the extreme pitches of the vibrato (on the condition that the vibrato is, in fact, even and does not stress certain frequencies by a jerky motion). It is wrong to think that the tone perceived is situated at the lower or the upper end of the vibrato range. An evenly vibrating tone is therefore perceived almost as much in tune, or out of tune, as a tone without vibrato.

An interesting experiment on the cello is to spread a fast sliding vibrato as far as a major second. Especially if the tone is *expected* (as in a scale), it will still be registered as the middle of the extreme, whining pitch range. If the upper and lower limits are then played separately, the listener is surprised to hear completely different pitches than he had perceived before. This ability of the ear to look for the geometric middle of the frequency ceases with an amplitude wider than a major second (as some singers occasionally use).

The amplitude of the vibrato depends not only on aesthetic considerations but also on the length of the string. A particular interval always implies the same ratio between the lengths of the string that produce the two pitches. A fourth above the first pitch always uses $\frac{3}{4}$ of the string length of the first pitch, no matter what absolute length the first pitch requires. A vibrato with a range of 5 millimeters ($\frac{1}{5}$ inch) changes the length of a string of 50 centimeters (20 inches) by $\frac{1}{100}$. If the string is only 25 centimeters (10 inches) long the same range of 5 millimeters changes the length by $\frac{1}{50}$. This means that for pitches an octave apart the vibrato for the high tone should use only half the amplitude of that of the lower tone to produce the same acoustic variation of pitch. The vibrato on a pitch two octaves higher should have only a fourth of the amplitude.

It is not always easy to control oneself in the heat of playing on stage, since there is an intimate connection between bodily exertion and degree of expressiveness. A strong sound is normally more expressive than a weak one insofar as it requires more energy to produce it, i.e., greater bow pressure. In addition we feel the need to vibrate more intensely on a loud sound. In the high positions, such a reaction may well lead to an amplitude that is too wide. One's need for expression may overrun one's alert aesthetic controls in intensive playing. (Even the aesthetic control of intonation may be overrun by this need of expression. Occasionally a string player with an indisputably good ear will not notice that he has played an entire passage too high, with all the pitches in the proper relationship to one another.)

Fortunately the technique of the cello provides a "brake" in the upper positions that does not let the vibrato get too wide. The movement is impeded somewhat by the thumb, which also presses down on the string. In addition, the angle formed by the axis of the hand and the fingerboard becomes more acute in the high positions. The component of the amplitude affecting the string is reduced because the hand vibrates in a more and more slanted position in relation to the fingerboard.

FIGURE 25

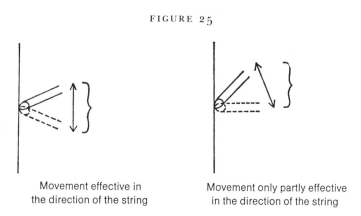

Movement effective in
the direction of the string

Movement only partly effective
in the direction of the string

The frequency of the vibrato should tend to be greater for high pitches than for low ones. It is not necessarily proportionate to the pitch, though, because that would make the vibrato for a high pitch extremely fast and shaky, which would make little aesthetic sense. (This effect can be heard if a tape is played at double speed.) But the density and brilliance of the high pitches as opposed to the low ones make the ear expect a similar density of vibrato.

Finally we need to mention the vibrato of the thumb itself. In general it is best to choose a fingering in which expressive tones are not played by the thumb, but it cannot always be avoided in complicated passages. The contact area of the thumb is quite narrow. In order to achieve a relatively wide vibrato the thumb must be rolled more strongly than, for example, the 1st finger. (A small wheel covers less distance per rotation.) Since the fingers are closer to the bridge than the thumb, the forearm axis is quite far from the rotational axis of the thumb. Therefore the entire arm would have to be rotated around the axis of the thumb, with considerable movement and expenditure of energy.

It is therefore advisable to move the other fingers from their normal position and bring them closer to the thumb for a longer thumb vibrato. The 1st finger can even be kept above the thumb, as in piano fingerings. In this way the forearm axis will approach that of the thumb and the energy expended will be reduced, thus making the rotation of the thumb easier and bigger.

When the other fingers vibrate, the thumb will normally stay on the string and accompany the vibrato movement elastically. In especially intensive vibrato, there is no objection to taking the thumb from the string temporarily in order to eliminate its braking effect. This is recommended only when the fingers are secure and the orientation on the fingerboard will not be disturbed. The same applies to the interval of a fourth between the 3rd finger and the thumb. In the highest positions it is uncomfortable to keep the thumb close to the other fingers; if it is not needed as a playing finger, it may be spread away from the 1st finger more than the interval of a second; possibly as much as a fourth.

Let us summarize:

1. Of the theoretically possible vibrato movements, the one created by upper arm rotation proves to be superior.

2. A very fast vibrato can be gained by a volar-dorsal movement of the wrist.

3. The widest rotational effect can be achieved by keeping the

contact place of the finger close to the extension of the fore-arm axis.

4. For double stops we may use the elasticity of the fingertips together with that of the joints.

5. A wide vibrato requires greater finger pressure (to create a greater frictional resistance on the fingerboard) than does a small one.

6. Accordingly, the thumb has to exert greater counterpressure to a big vibrato than to a small one (in the lower positions). It is as nearly opposite the vibrating finger as is comfortable.

7. The pitch perceived by the listener is the midpoint of the extremes of the vibrato amplitude.

8. The shorter the string the narrower the amplitude of the vibrato must be in order to maintain the same range in pitch.

9. A somewhat faster vibrato is more satisfying aesthetically for high pitches than for lower ones.

Part Three

THE BOW

VIII

THE BOWED STRING

How Is a Sound Produced on the String?

THE READER should not be frightened by this question for we will not discuss acoustics in detail in this book. But many questions about the production of sound can be answered with the help of a few simple natural laws. It should become superfluous to say, "This is a matter of opinion," a phrase that is still often used with respect to sound production.

Let us recall first of all the image of a vibrating open string in a simplified schematic presentation (Fig. 26). We see that the largest amplitude of the string is in the middle. It decreases toward

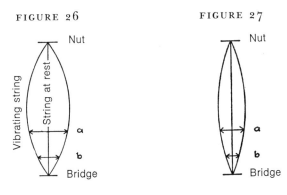

FIGURE 26   FIGURE 27

115

both ends to the point where it disappears completely at the nut and at the bridge. To put it differently, the amplitude reaches its maximum at the middle; at both ends of the string it is zero.

Since the frequency of a certain sound is the same at every point on the string, it is obvious that point *a*, close to the middle of the string, must have a greater velocity per vibration than does point *b*, which is close to the bridge, since *a* must travel farther than *b* to complete one vibration. In addition we can deduce that both the point close to the bridge and the one far away from it must travel farther at a large amplitude of the entire string than at a small one (Fig. 27). Traveling farther means greater velocity. If we disregard the section of the string between the nut and the middle, which is not used by the bow, we may say the following:

1. The velocity of a point close to the bridge is lower than that of a point farther away from the bridge.

2. The vibrating velocity of any point on the string is greater the larger the amplitude of the string.

Both of these facts will play an important part in all considerations of sound production.*

We all know that the string is made to vibrate by the bow's going across it. Why is that? We could conceive of the possibility that the friction of the bow pulls the string to one side at the point of friction, as in Fig. 28. The string would have the effect of a tightened spring, and the friction (which is the same at any point of the bow hair) would pull the string at the contact point as far as the spring would permit. And in fact, if we were to use a different material for the friction, for instance, rubber, the same

---

* A simplified illustration of these considerations will suffice here. According to Wilhelm Trendelenburg's observations of the different velocities of the string at the contact point of the bow for the two phases of vibration, it is clear that the string in reality vibrates in an extremely complex pattern. We can disregard these observations, since they have no effect on our practical playing.

FIGURE 28

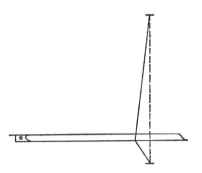

effect would take place. No vibration would result and therefore no sound.

The material we use, horsehair with rosin, however, has peculiar characteristics. Its degree of friction changes, and we can discern two kinds of friction, whose strength is different:

1. *Static friction,* when the string clings firmly to the hair as if "glued."

2. *Sliding friction,* when the string slides along the hair.

Static friction is much greater than sliding friction. For example, if the brakes of a car are slammed on, all four wheels will lock, and the braking effect will be noticeably less than if the brake is pushed down only to the point where the wheels can just turn. (Hence the brakes of some cars are constructed in a way that they cannot lock.)

When the bow is moved across the string the hair "clings" to the string and pulls it along to the side. The "spring" is tightened. The hair, however, pulls further; the tension of the string becomes so great that it cannot "cling" to the hair any longer. At this point the hair "slides" across the string; the static friction thus changes

into sliding friction. The latter is so small that the string recoils
to its initial position with so much impetus that it swings past its
point of rest to a position as far to the other side as the point at
which the static friction stopped. From there it swings back toward
its point of rest, which is a medium position between the two extremes. At this moment the contact point moves with a speed
roughly equal to that of the hair, which has by now moved on, and
another phase of static friction starts. This process is repeated in
accordance with the length and tension of the string (see Fig. 29).

FIGURE 29

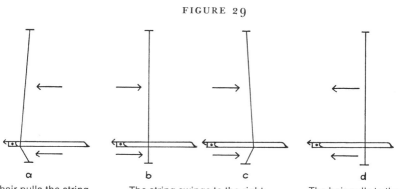

a

The hair pulls the string
to the left: static friction.

b

The string swings to the right;
the hair pulls to the left:
sliding friction.

c

d

The hair pulls to the left;
the string swings to the le
again static friction.

Another question arises: Could it be possible that the frequency of the above process depends on the degree of friction of
the hair? The intrinsic frequency of the string is so pronounced
that it will always prevail over the friction. The intrinsic laws of
the string are of such strength that the string instantly creates its
own vibrating pattern, which has the largest amplitude in the
middle, even though the point of stimulation may be in the lowest
eighth of its length. It does not vibrate as shown in Fig. 30a but as
in Fig. 30b.

FIGURE 30

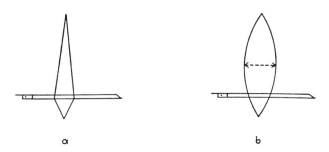

a   b

Change of Volume: Pressure, Speed, and Contact Point*

We can say that a sound is louder the larger the amplitude of the string. How then can we influence the amplitude of the string in order to play softly or loudly?

It is unnecessary to prove with exact physics that the hair of the bow sticks to the string more firmly the more strongly the hair is pressed against it. Friction increases with pressure. Therefore we must formulate the following rule, with some reservations:

> In order to achieve a loud sound the pressure on the string must increase.

No concept in the entire string pedagogy is as misused and full of negative associations as *pressing*. From the facts given above we can only come to this conclusion: The greater the pressure the greater the adhesion of the string to the bow. The greater the adhesion the farther the bow pulls the string aside and the larger the amplitude and, therefore, the volume.

---

* A detailed schematic presentation of the mutual interdependence of pressure, speed, and contact point can be found in *Die Klanggestaltung auf Streichinstrumenten* (Sound Production on String Instruments) by Margarete Hopfer (Leipzig: Kistner & Siegel, 1941), which is based on experiments by August Eichhorn [Mantel's highly esteemed teacher].

So far we have looked at one individual vibration of the string. Let us follow this vibrating process farther now. The string is pulled to the left and then recoils to the right to the opposite position; from there it swings back to the left without additional help from the friction. Now the direction of the vibration is the same as that of the bow. At the moment when the string again sticks to the hair the vibrating energy of the string is added to the static friction of the hair. This process of energy augmentation is repeated during several vibrations until a certain amplitude is reached that cannot be surpassed at a specific pressure because of the increased tension of the string at both extreme points. The velocity of the string in full vibration is therefore greater than that of the first vibration. From this fact we can draw certain conclusions for our examination of the problems of how to make a string speak.

If the pressure is increased still more the following happens: The string is pulled farther to the left (Fig. 29), thus increasing the velocity of vibration. It swings to the right and then back to the left (in the direction of the bow) at that increased speed. Since the velocity of the string is now greater than the speed of the bow the string is slowed down to the speed of the bow in the following phase. In addition to the slowing down caused by the sliding friction during the sliding phase of the vibration we thus encounter another braking effect that could be avoided. An increase in amplitude is thus impeded even though the pressure increases, and the sound does not become louder but weaker.

Besides the fundamental vibration of the string (which has its largest amplitude in the middle of the string), there is a series of partial vibrations. Vibrating "knots" are formed, which divide the length of the string into halves, thirds, fourths, etc., of its length. These partial vibrations, or overtones, are responsible for the timbre of every instrument because of their respective strength in relation to one another; the less they are hindered from developing, the more colorful and resonant and, therefore, the more brilliant the sound becomes.

To avoid the slowdown in the static friction phase and the resulting weakened sound, the speed of the bow must be increased when the pressure is increased. The relationship between the two will be correct again; the speed of the hair will correspond to the increased velocity of the vibrations.

In this process the extreme elasticity of the hair plays an important part. If the hair were a rigid object the static friction phase would be very short; both speeds could, so to speak, be equal at only a single point of a particular vibration. Therefore the stick of the bow, even with rosin on it, cannot manage to set the string in full vibration. Only overtones will result, creating an unpleasant glassy sound, which, of course, might be used occasionally as a special effect. However, the hair, whose length may be stretched, follows the string at the contact point for a little longer. Thus the path of the hair is not identical with that of the stick. While the latter performs an even movement, the hair travels in little thrusts in rhythm with the vibrations of the string, thus extending the static friction phase. The elasticity of the bow also has its role; it must complement the elasticity of the hair, but it should not be too soft either, lest it blunt the delicate impulses initiated by the hand.

Now we can complete the statement about pressure:

In order to achieve a greater volume the pressure on the string and the speed of the bow must be simultaneously increased.

In the beginning of this chapter we saw that the velocity of the vibrations decreases as we approach the bridge. This fact can be used to advantage. Instead of increasing the speed when increasing the pressure and thus adjusting the speed of the bow to the velocity of the string, the bow may be moved closer to the bridge, where the string vibrates more slowly. Since the velocity of vibration of the string during the static friction phase must be adjusted to the speed of the bow, the same effect can be achieved either by increasing the speed of the bow or by changing the contact to a point where the velocity is less.

Now we can summarize the conditions for varying the volume in a final statement:

> In order to achieve greater volume it is necessary to exert greater pressure on the string. At the same time either the speed of the bow must be increased or the contact point must be shifted closer to the bridge.

Now let us assume that we are forced to change the speed of the bow. We can easily deduce what will happen from what we have learned so far: If the speed is increased too much the hair will slide across the string in the first phase of vibration. No static friction is therefore possible, and the string is only minimally pulled to the side by the sliding friction. The energy provided by the sliding friction is too small to create a fundamental vibration, and only the weaker overtones will start to sound. The string does not speak—it squeals and whistles (the occasionally used "ponticello" effect).

There are two possible ways of preventing this from happening:

1. Increase the pressure. As a result, the static friction will increase and the string will be "handled more firmly" and pulled farther to the side. It will have sufficient energy to vibrate in its entirety, but the amplitude will be higher and the sound therefore louder.

2. Look for a place where the velocity of vibration at the contact point is the same as the speed of the bow. Since the velocity of vibration increases with the distance from the bridge, the situation

can be corrected by shifting the contact point toward the fingerboard. By this means the sound level will remain the same without the necessity of increasing the pressure.

Let us summarize the conditions for changing the speed of the bow:

A higher bow speed requires either increased pressure, which makes the sound louder, or a shift of the contact point toward the fingerboard.

The reverse is true if the speed of the bow is decreased. The phenomenon described above results: The speed of the bow, being too slow, slows down the string in the static friction phase, producing a weak sound. Thus a speed that is too slow means *relatively* too great a pressure. To correct a speed that is too slow either decrease the pressure or move closer to the bridge, where the string vibrates more slowly.

Finally let us consider the case in which it is necessary to change the contact point. First, let us move the contact point in the direction of the bridge while maintaining a constant pressure and speed of the bow. The velocity of the string will become slower than the speed of the bow so that we again lack static friction. There are now two possibilities for compensating: either slow down the bow so that it fits the changed circumstances or increase the pressure (which in turn increases the amplitude).

In the opposite situation, when the contact point is moved toward the fingerboard, the velocity of the vibrating contact point is greater and the bow must be moved faster in order to maintain the same volume and to avoid the braking effect during each phase of static friction. Or, we can diminish the pressure so that the velocity of the string again corresponds to the speed of the bow. In this case a lower volume will be the result.

Let us summarize the conditions for changing the contact point:

If the contact point is shifted toward the bridge either the speed of the bow must be diminished or the pressure must be increased; in the latter case the volume will also increase. Shifting toward the fingerboard has the opposite effects.

These rules are the logical consequence of the fact that the speed of the bow must correspond to the velocity of vibration at the contact point.

There is yet another conclusion that can be drawn from these facts. So far we have not mentioned the degree to which the con-

FIGURE 31

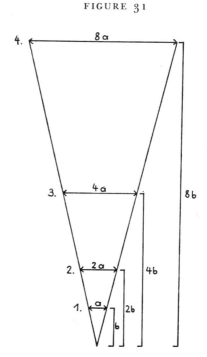

a: Amplitude. Also velocity of string and speed of bow. b: Distance from bridge

tact point and the speed must be matched. If we play a certain tone and double the speed of the bow, according to our experiments the velocity of the string must also be doubled. This means that, if the pressure is to be kept constant throughout both the initial speed and its doubling, we must look for a contact point that vibrates at a velocity twice that of the initial tone. Where is that contact point?

Fig. 31 is an attempt to represent schematically the section of a vibrating string in which the bow is ordinarily used. The vertex at the bottom corresponds to the bridge, and the horizontal line at the top corresponds to the point at which the string passes over the lower edge of the fingerboard. The horizontal lines *a, 2a, 4a, 8a* represent the amplitudes at the distances *b, 2b, 4b, 8b*, respectively, from the bridge. (The sides of the angle in the diagram should really be two shallow curves, but to simplify matters we will regard them as straight lines.) The distance between the two sides of an angle increases in proportion to the distance from the vertex. That means that the speed of the bow must change in proportion to the distance from the bridge, provided that the pressure, i.e., the volume, stays the same.

> If the speed is doubled, the distance from the bridge must also be doubled; if it is cut in half, the distance from the bridge must also be cut in half.*

Let us then summarize: Each change of one of the three factors—pressure, speed, and contact point—must be compensated for by a change in at least one of the other two factors:

---

* The relationship among the distances from the bridge are slightly simplified in the diagram. Close to the bridge there is another factor of increasing influence—the "lever" with which the full amplitude of the middle of the string must be provoked becomes shorter and shorter and therefore less favorable. The distances from the bridge in Fig. 31 therefore do not relate quite as 1:2:4:8; in reality the points are slightly closer to one another.

1. With a change in volume (pressure):
   a. the speed must change while the contact point stays the same, or
   b. the contact point must change while the speed stays the same.
2. With a change in speed:
   a. the contact point must change while the volume stays the same, or
   b. the volume must change while the contact point stays the same.
3. With a change in contact point:
   a. the speed must change while the volume stays the same, or
   b. the volume must change while the speed stays the same.

One more observation must be made. The comparable contact points of all four strings are not the same. On the lower strings they are somewhat closer to the fingerboard than on the higher strings. This is true not only at the moment when the bow is started, when the process of vibration begins. (There it would be plausible that the greater mass of the lower strings would need to be started at a more advantageous point, i.e., one closer to the middle of the string.) It is also true that with an already vibrating lower string the optimal and freely vibrating sound is produced farther from the bridge than on the A string.

If our theory that the speed of the bow must correspond to the velocity of vibration is correct, then the lower strings must have a lower velocity in the static friction phase than do the higher ones. The explanation that a lower frequency also means a lower velocity is not sufficient, since (at a given volume) the amplitude of the lower strings is several times as large as that of the higher strings. The volume perceived seems approximately proportionate to the total energy output of a string, that is, to the product of frequency and amplitude.

In that context we can make another observation: Our examinations above have presupposed that a large amplitude creates a loud sound and a small amplitude a soft sound. Let us now perform an experiment on the C string (where we can observe this phenomenon especially well). Let us create an extremely wide fundamental vibration of about one inch. This sound will seem softer than one that is created closer to the bridge with greater pressure and a visibly smaller amplitude. The latter sound is much more colorful. Therefore we must conclude that the volume of a sound is not determined by the amplitude of the fundamental vibration alone, but by the entire energy output, which includes that of all the overtones.

Of course, it is impossible in practical playing to stick to one particular contact point or speed for a certain sound. Musical phrasings almost never require as even a course of sound as we are dealing with here. What is decisive, however, is that, since we know the basic relationships, we have an explanation for the physical causes of certain kinds of unsatisfying sound, and after a while certain tendencies will become second nature as we play:

1. Loud sounds are played closer to the bridge.
2. Long sounds are played closer to the bridge.
3. The higher strings are played closer to the bridge.

Sound Colors

With reference to shaping a piece of music we often use *color nuances, shadings,* and similar terms. In general, they refer to the various dynamic possibilities of the instrument that give a phrase meaning, relief, or *color.* Often the term *color* is used to denote a performance that is lively in all its details. In this sense a musical phrase will have a different color when played with a wide range of dynamics and with a wide vibrato than when played with an even volume and with perhaps an intensive, narrow vibrato. One may be just as good as the other; the listener will have the impression of a different coloring. Here we will limit the term *sound color* to mean an audible difference in the same tone with the same volume.

For the systematic representation of the dynamic possibilities of sound production we presupposed that an "optimal" sound is desired, i.e., a sound that neither is restricted in its spectrum of overtones by too much pressure nor runs the danger of not speaking properly because of too little pressure.

Now we will go one step further. In reality, the range for the production of a satisfying sound is fortunately not as narrow as this system may suggest. Without questioning the basic validity of the principle, we must admit that there is a certain amount of tolerance in applying pressure to the string. For instance, we may use borderline sounds, those that have a little too much pressure in relation to the speed and the contact point. These sounds will be weaker than the "optimal" ones and must be employed only when a certain effect is required. However, we must be especially cautious when teaching such sounds. An unsatisfactory sound quality cannot be justified afterwards by calling it intentional. The same goes for sounds that lie in the dangerous realm of relatively too little pressure. Their diagnosis, however, is simpler since they turn into a "ponticello" effect at a specific degree of excess speed or insufficient pressure. At this limit the string either speaks or does not. However, on the side of too much pressure the sound gradually loses its brilliance to the point (which can be reached only by force) at which the string is completely choked. In this way the sound first changes its frequency and finally does not sound at all.

Thus the available scale of sound colors ranges from a glassy ponticello effect (without fundamental vibration) to a choked sound. We may regulate these colors

1. by changing *only* the bow pressure, or
2. by changing *only* the speed, or
3. by changing *only* the contact point.

In addition to changing the relative pressure, there is another way of influencing the overtone pattern. An "optimal" sound produced at the fingerboard is basically different from one produced at the bridge. Near the bridge the sounds are richer in overtones and therefore more colorful than those in the middle of the string. (On the guitar, where there is no problem of muting a sound by the friction of the bow, an especially brilliant sound can be created by plucking close to the bridge.)

An "optimal sound—a colorful one, rich in overtones—must be played as close to the bridge as is possible at the chosen dynamic level and bow speed. Or more simply: a brilliant sound is played closer to the bridge.

From Fig. 31 we may conclude that deviating from the "optimal" contact point is more serious the closer the bow is to the bridge. At contact point *4.* a deviation of as much as the distance *b* means that the bow will reach a contact point at which the string vibrates only slightly slower, but a deviation of *b* at *1.* will move the bow on *top* of the bridge. That is why the beginner prefers to play midway between the bridge and the fingerboard. In fact, he will tend to play close to the fingerboard, where small deviations make little difference. If the contact point changes by an inch or so the change in sound is not disastrous, but a brilliant sound cannot be achieved in this way. For this reason we must insist that a player learn to stay at a chosen contact point without accidentally deviating from it.

Speed, Pressure, and Contact Point in Their Practical Application

In previous discussions we have surveyed the physical basis of sound production on our instrument. On the one hand we have a variety of means at our disposal: a choice of all the contact points on the string between the fingerboard and the immediate vicinity of the bridge; a full range of speeds, from a long, sustained sound to one for which the bow must fly swiftly across the string from frog to tip; and every degree of pressure, from a massive fortissimo to a thin pianissimo in which the bow hardly touches the string. On the other hand, in applying these means we are bound by strict rules. We may "do as we please," but having decided on a certain volume, duration, and sound color, we must stick to the laws of creating such a sound if we wish to realize our conception of it.

So far we have assumed that we are dealing with open strings. If the string is now shortened by the left hand, the entire system of contact points shifts toward the bridge in proportion to the amount of shortening. For instance, for an octave shift on one string (the octave cuts the string in half), the appropriate contact point for the upper tone will be half as far from the bridge *relative* to where it should be, and the sound will be choked.

There is a problem in trying to shift the contact point closer to the bridge quickly (in order to maintain the tone quality of the previous contact point). To make the adjustment from the lower tone to the higher one exclusively by shifting the contact point necessitates an abrupt sliding motion with the bow at the same moment as the left hand shifts. An offensive noise will result, and the contact between the bow and the string will be severed at this moment.

Another way of making the adjustment is to keep the bow at the previous contact point and double its speed. The contact between the bow and the string will be guaranteed even during the shift, but one may be forced to use a lot of bow for the new speed. This method will not be very practical if the new tone is to be relatively long. A combination of both processes is therefore the solution. One gradually approaches the new contact point while still on the lower tone, slowing down the bow proportionately. At the moment of the shift no abrupt change of contact point takes place; instead one uses a higher bow speed on the higher tone. The bow continues to slide gradually toward the bridge, while its speed is again reduced proportionately. Since, in principle, each tone has its own system of contact points on the string, this process is continually applied. Eventually, of course, this process happens unconsciously.

There is still another way of making the shift without affecting the sound quality—by playing the higher of the two tones at a lower volume. In fact, we can observe this technique in many cellists, who may even believe that they *want* to play the higher tone more softly. In reality their interpretation has been influenced by the conditions of their instrument. Similar conditions apply if we have the rhythm shown in Fig. 32.

FIGURE 32

There are two possible ways of playing this succession of notes without affecting the sound quality:

1. Simply play the up bow very loudly (one of the most persistent habits, and one not limited to beginners).

2. Shift the contact point of the up bow away from the bridge, applying the combination of a shift in the contact point and a change in the speed. At the end of the dotted half note the bow is already approaching the fingerboard; at the beginning of the quarter note it moves still farther and accelerates greatly. At the end of the quarter note apply the reverse procedure.

The possibilities for a good crescendo are very similar. The pressure must increase, as we know. In compensation we can

1. gradually slide closer to the bridge, or
2. increase the speed along with the pressure, and
3. gradually increase the speed as well as the pressure and at the same time approach the bridge.

The third possibility is probably the most advisable. For a diminuendo the reverse procedure applies.

There is another possibility for a diminuendo that is a special case beyond the stated principles, especially when a sound is allowed to "die out." Once the string is vibrating at full amplitude the pressure can be reduced gradually *without* decreasing the speed in exact proportion. Since the string will have enough vibrating energy left and will want to remain in this state, it is not necessary to try to create static friction for each vibration in a rapid diminuendo. Even if the speed of the bow is somewhat greater than that of the string, the latter will maintain its fundamental vibration. However, starting the string with the same relatively light pressure will result in a ponticello effect: The string will not speak.

When applying the principles of sound production to practical playing, we have an immense number of possible combinations for just a simple stroke. When the varied dynamics of musical phrasings are added, it is impossible to describe the process of even a single stroke of the bow with any exactness. But it should be remembered that each of the possibilities obeys physical laws.

To complete the list of difficulties we face in understanding these instrumental processes there is one aspect that lies beyond the limits of exact description. It appears that, the validity of the above interrelations notwithstanding, the instrument does not always react according to our expectations. The resonance conditions within the structure of the instrument and the material it is made of favor certain sounds and hinder others. The most extreme case is the well-known wolf sound, which on many instruments can only be avoided by consciously pressing too hard. Also, different cellos have different resonance conditions, as one discovers when one plays an unfamiliar instrument. Sounds that respond to relatively little pressure on one's own instrument will not speak; others, which one is used to attacking harder in order to get them to vibrate "optimally," are dimmed by what is, relatively speaking, too much pressure. An unfamiliar instrument not only sounds different but also "feels" different; it therefore takes a while for the motor impulses to adjust to the new conditions.

Our goal when practicing must be the eventual ability of the body to translate sound conceptions into the appropriate, mutually interdependent movements without having to make a detour through the consciousness. For that purpose, the ear needs a clear conception of the sound. This conception in turn can be achieved more easily if we know the means to realize it and can follow this route consciously whenever necessary.

A clear conception of the "ideal" sound can be achieved more easily if this sound is the rule and not the exception. Some players seem content if the sound does not show any disturbing noises at the upper end (ponticello) or at the lower end (with too much pressure) of the color scale. The sound is "beautiful" merely in the sense of "not ugly." We can only train our capacities if we approach their limits again and again. The means should not be left to chance, however; they must be chosen consciously. Irrational concepts of sound production may perhaps produce an "ideal" sound in a lucky moment, but this luck cannot become a method.

Incorrect motor conceptions are almost more destructive than ignorance of these complex relations. They will contradict what the player does in reality and what he feels. This contradiction of the ideas and the sensations will have disastrous effects on the body: The discrepancy between the conception of a movement and the movement itself leads to the wrong muscle activity, discomfort, and muscular tightness.

It is disturbing to hear that certain string players still believe that forte is played with all the hair of the bow, piano with little, i.e., with a slanted bow. Quite apart from the fact that, with a certain amount of pressure, all the hair inevitably touches the string, a simple experiment shows that no change in volume occurs when playing with little or with all the hair at a certain pressure. Many years of daily practice should have revealed this fact. If the instrument is placed on the floor and only the weight of the bow itself is used, first with the bow tilted and then held flat, no difference in sound can be detected, except for a minimal increase in the mere noise of the bow. (The latter, of course, plays a certain role in the color of the cello sound, but can hardly be influenced by the player.)

The author attaches importance to the tilting of the bow only insofar as comfortable playing is concerned. When the bow is perpendicular to the string, the wrist must be lifted uncomfortably high, otherwise the right hand will have an insecure grip on the frog. Only for off-the-string bowings would this flat position occasionally be of use since it increases the rebound of the bow. It might also be useful occasionally to tilt the bow extremely when playing pianissimo and use "less hair," since a smaller amount of hair is more elastic. If the right hand is in danger of trembling because of nervousness, the tilting of the bow acts as a shock absorber and prevents audible irregularities of sound.

Problems of Sound Production: How to Make a String Speak

Until now we have examined the problems that arise in connection with the vibrating string *during* the course of vibration. We have ignored what happens at the *beginning* of a tone, that is, during the short moment between the time the string leaves its position of rest and the time it reaches its full amplitude. The quality at the beginning of a tone is not identical with that of the full sound; a tone may start out "scratchy" but may be ideal during its course. Another tone that is not noisy at the beginning may turn out to be weak in sound. (The following discussion refers only to the production of a single bow stroke; special conditions encountered in the bow change will be treated in succeeding chapters.)

Independent of the quality of the sound during its course, the choice of expressive means for the beginning of a tone ranges from an inaudible "stealing" into the sound to an aggressive "consonantal" or "plosive" beginning, comparable to a spoken hard *p;* below this scale we find the whistling sound, which starts with too little pressure, above it the scratchy sound, which can only develop into a full sound after a few choked vibrations have passed.

There are two basically different ways of setting a string in vibration from its position of rest:

1. The string is pulled out of its position of rest and then released; it continues to vibrate by itself until it has passed its vibrating energy on to the air. The clearest case of this kind of attack is the pizzicato; its beginning is a sharp plosive sound.

2. The string reaches its full amplitude by adding the small amounts of energy that develop in each individual phase of static

friction to the already accumulated energy. The most typical case of this kind is the phenomenon of *resonance:* If there are two strings of the same pitch in the same room, when one is played or plucked, the other will vibrate as a result of the minimal impulses which the air transmits within "earshot" and which add up to a certain amplitude. It is easy to perform this experiment on the cello; in this case additional small mechanical energy impulses are at work, which are transmitted by the bridge and the nut.

In the first kind of attack, the bow takes over the role of the pizzicato finger. As described earlier, it rests on the string with a predetermined pressure, then starts moving and pulls the string along. In this first vibration of the sound, at the point where the string slides off the hair and the static friction stops, the full vibrating velocity has already been reached.* In order to equal this velocity the bow must also be accelerated to its full speed with a jerk. Even if this speed is not especially great the resulting jerk is considerable. The natural process for the arm, however, is to accelerate gradually. No object can be brought to a specific speed without a phase of acceleration. The heavier the object the more gradual is its acceleration with a given energy; much more energy is needed for the same amount of acceleration of a heavy object than for a light one. Since the right arm weighs several kilograms, considerable energy is required to accelerate it with a jerk. (Even a powerful racing car needs several seconds to accelerate from 0 to 50 mph.) It is advisable to make the relatively light hand and the very light fingers participate actively in the accelerating process. The first jerk of the acceleration can be taken care of by the fingers and the hand, while the heavier arm gains time to accelerate more gradually.

---

* Even in this case several vibrations are necessary before the full amplitude of the *entire* string is reached; this process takes so little time, however, that we cannot influence it consciously.

The second problem is that once in motion, the arm will tend to continue to accelerate. Consider it as a kind of pendulum: A pendulum reaches its greatest speed in the vertical position; at both extremes of the amplitude its speed is zero. Gravity makes the pendulum accelerate evenly until it reaches the vertical position, and then slows it down just as evenly as the pendulum moves upward. The arm also has the tendency to accelerate at the beginning and to slow down at the end of each bow stroke. (This fact will play an important role in the bow change.)

Since, in a hard attack, the full speed of the bow is already reached at the beginning of the tone we must watch that the speed does not increase further—unless the pressure also increases, although this is rarely applicable in short notes with a plosive start.

The situation is different for the second kind of attack. The bow touches the string with minimal pressure and starts moving. The gradual acceleration, which comes naturally to the arm, is exactly what is needed for this type of attack. The active help of the hand and the fingers can be dispensed with. The pressure must increase parallel with the bow speed until the string has reached its full amplitude. If the pressure does not increase in proportion to the increasing speed, there will be a whistling noise and the familiar situation of the speed of the bow being too great for the vibrating velocity of the string and the string not speaking.

This process of accelerating while simultaneously increasing the pressure should normally happen in a very short time. If the process takes too long each tone will start with a crescendo, which is of little use for phrasing. Even though this kind of playing is free of side noises it eventually becomes monotonous because it uses the same expressive means over and over again.

The problem with the second kind of attack, however, is to keep the speed and the pressure in the correct relationship to each other: Great acceleration requires a large increase in pressure; little acceleration requires little increase. In practice, in attempting to avoid breaking this law in one direction or the other (i.e., too great an increase in pressure *or* too great an increase in speed) one may easily commit the opposite offense.

For the player the two kinds of attack have quite different sensations. For the hard attack a great deal of energy is necessary at the outset, but it must be reduced immediately. To use the example of a car again, to reach the speed of 50 mph as fast as possible the driver must press the gas pedal all the way to the floor even if the motor is very powerful. When this speed is reached the driver may turn off the motor, and the car will continue to run at the same speed for a while. Turning off the motor—in our case, releasing the musculature that moves the arm—must happen very consciously because otherwise still further acceleration will be the result and the string will not speak.

Another problem is that a hard attack is often required for a short note. Despite the great initial acceleration we must use less bow for the duration of the note than for a soft tone that swells gradually. Failure to use less bow is a frequent mistake in executing this attack, for a hard attack is usually associated with a loud sound, and for a loud sound we are used to employing a lot of bow.

For a soft attack things are somewhat simpler, since the more gradual acceleration corresponds more to the natural pendulum movement of the arm. A soft attack is often combined with a longer tone. The initial speed is less but the following crescendo uses more bow than does a sound that starts plosively and has the same rhythmic duration. It pays therefore to understand this paradox: hard attack—less bow, soft attack—more bow. It seems to contradict our discussion of sound production, namely, that a loud sound needs more bow than does a soft one. (The sections on staccato and spiccato will deal with the physical execution of these bowings.)

So far we have examined the two extreme modes of attack. It would be nice if we had to practice only those two. But again, we mostly use a synthesis of the two in our playing, i.e., a certain amount of predetermined pressure and an additional increase in speed until the full amplitude is reached. The attack characterizes the music. The beginning of a sound, regardless of the instrument, gives each tone its own individuality. If the beginning of a tone is cut from a tape recording it is difficult to identify the instrument, for the beginning of a tone is more characteristic of the instrument (and of the music) than the further course of its vibrations.

Since in many cases defective attacks are caused by too much acceleration (and too little increase in pressure), we might reduce the total speed of the stroke, i.e., play with less bow. And, in fact, a succession of short notes may be improved in this way. However, the impression of such a passage is paler and often objectively softer.

There is a better means of improving the attack in such passages. Imagine the vibrating string as a lever with its pivot at the bridge. This lever is harder to move the closer to the pivot the force is applied. At the bridge it cannot be moved at all; at the point with the largest amplitude, in the middle of the string, it could be moved most easily. A point far from the bridge will therefore offer less resistance to the applied force than one closer to the bridge; thus conditions at the more distant point are better for the attack. In an attack at the bridge the overtones are so strong that they endanger the fundamental vibration. (In reality the overtones are created before the mechanical influence of the bow extends to the entire elastic string and allows the fundamental to sound. The details of the processes of initiating a sound are extremely complicated; here we must limit ourselves to the aspects that are of practical importance.

In order to produce the desired fundamental as fast as possible in short single notes it is advisable to move farther from the bridge than is usual in normal legato playing. The learned habit of playing as close as possible to the bridge in order to achieve a brilliant sound may prevent us from making exceptions to the rule when required. However, by being conscious of these rules we can learn to react to them. This is one case where indefatigable practicing alone will not solve the problem.

Let us now examine the difference between a hard and a soft attack with respect to the playing sensations, for example, in a sequence of short but ringing notes at the balance point of the bow:

1. For a hard attack the pressure must be predetermined, that is, in addition to the actual playing impulse, we need a "pressure impulse" without any movement of the bow. We sense it in the manner shown in Fig. 33. The pressure is set during the rests. The

FIGURE 33

P M PM PM PM

P: Pressure, M: Movement

movement itself must be abrupt. The hand and the fingers as well as the arm are used actively.

2. For a soft attack the pressure need not be predetermined, nothing happens in the rests, and the pressure and the movement are integrated. Instead we see that the natural pendulum movement of the arm is *not* enhanced by the hand and fingers as in a hard attack; otherwise the acceleration would be too great and the string would not speak well. This means that the hand and the fingers must not make *any* movement of their own.

As a marginal note we might add that we often look for the cause of a poor attack in the bow when in truth it is the left hand that is at fault; it may prevent the string from reaching its full amplitude because the fingers are not pressing the string down hard enough.

In addition, we must concede that there are a few insoluble problems that cannot be rationalized. Several factors may influence the attack: The tensions between the sound post and the bridge may be incorrect (a violin maker may be able to help with that); often a new string will change matters surprisingly; and the weather, with its varying humidity, influences the sound.

The beginning of a sound is even more sensitive to an incorrect contact point than the sustained sound is; at a point at which the sustained sound shows only a slight disturbance, the string may not respond at all to an attack. Once the string is vibrating at its full amplitude, it tends to maintain this state, in accordance with the laws of inertia; minor mistakes are not as grave as they are when the string leaves its position of rest and starts to vibrate.

In order to translate all this knowledge of the physical facts into automatic bodily impulses, we must conceptualize and feel a clear distinction between pressure, speed, and acceleration. Especially for an experienced player who is used to matching the differences in pressure by changes of speed, it is not easy to separate these components consciously. But a player who believes that bow speed requires no previous acceleration will try in vain to achieve a soft, bell-like stroke at the balance point of the bow.

IX

TRANSMISSION
OF PRESSURE
TO THE STRING

Arm Weight

HOW TO transmit the weight of the arm to the string need not be a matter of speculation. A few considerations on the mechanism of a lever can help solve the problems involved. Let us start with a primitive experiment. Using two rubber bands, fasten a long pencil to the tray of a letter scale in such a way that the pencil sticks out on one side. Place a weight of 90 grams (3 ounces) on the scale. If the pencil weighs 10 grams (½ ounce), it and the weight together total 100 grams (3½ ounces) (Fig. 34a). Now suspend the weight from the far end of the pencil. The scale, of course, shows the same weight—100 grams (Fig. 34b).

Let us now apply this principle to the bow (we will ignore the slanted position of the instrument for the time being):

The vertical pressure on the string (which corresponds to the total weight on the scale) is identical to the vertical pressure of the arm (which corresponds to the weight) plus the weight of the bow (which corresponds to the pencil), *no matter at which point of the bow this pressure is applied to the string.*

FIGURE 34

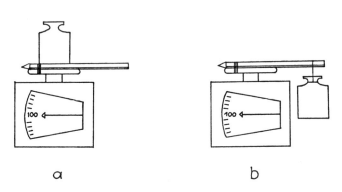

a   b

The arm has considerable weight. Let us assume that the part of the arm close to the hand (the remaining part is held up by the shoulder) weighs about 2 kilograms (5 lb), and let us disregard the changes in weight created by the various angles formed by the arm and the body. This means that about 2 kilograms press on the string if the whole arm is used. That much pressure is not necessary even for a brutal sforzato at the frog; any additional active pressure from the arm will be totally superfluous. We cannot really speak of arm pressure in the sense of active participation. If the arm, which weighs 2 kilograms, rests on the string with about 0.5 kilograms of pressure, 1.5 kilograms of arm weight still remains. If the string is pressed down with 300 grams of weight, there remains 1.7 kilograms of arm weight, which the muscles must actively carry. The tension and pressure scales in Fig. 35 illustrate this principle.

Now we can formulate the following statement:

The musculature holding up the arm is relieved of the
amount of pressure that rests on the string; the louder the
sound the more relaxed this musculature will be.

FIGURE 35

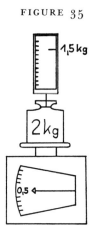

This rule is easily demonstrated: If the frog of the bow is placed on
the string and the arm is completely relaxed, an unnecessary
amount of pressure is resting on the string. To diminish this pressure we must use the musculature that holds up the arm. This
fact alone shows us how cautious we must be with words like
relaxation. If one is forced to practice pianissimo for an extended
length of time (perhaps because the neighbors are asleep), the arm
tires much faster than in loud playing because the muscles must
actively hold up the entire arm, including the bow.

We will now proceed to the variable force required to transmit this partial arm weight.

Moment of Rotation (Rotational Force)

If the rubber bands in Fig. 34 are not too tight, the situation
depicted in Fig. 36 will result. The combined weight of the two

objects is still 100 grams, but the weight tends to make the pencil rotate around point *P*. It is obvious that this rotation will be stronger the heavier the weight.

FIGURE 36

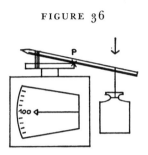

Let us now turn the experiment upside down, as in Fig. 37. Instead of the weight pressing down, we have the resistance of the string, which presses up. We can say that the pressure exerted on the string is identical to the resistance with which the string meets it. If the letter scale were able to register zero grams when turned upside down, showing that no force is pressing it down, it will register 90 grams if, together with the 10 grams of the pencil, a pressure of 100 grams is to rest on the string.

FIGURE 37

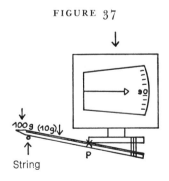

This last experiment reproduces the exact conditions created when the bow transmits pressure to the string. The greater the total pressure transmitted via the upside-down scale down onto the string the greater the rotating effect on the pencil, the further the rubber band expands, and the stronger the rubber band has to be to prevent this rotation.

Translated into cello technique this means: The greater the vertical pressure of the arm (i.e., perpendicular to the plane of the string) and the greater the weight of the arm resting on the string, the greater the force of the rotating mechanism must be to transmit this pressure onto the string. (For modifications that result from slanting the instrument see p. 160). Forearm rotation (pronation) is just such a rotating mechanism. The force of this mechanism is called *moment of rotation* or *rotational force*. If the rotational force of the pronation falls short of matching the vertical force of the arm, the arm will press the frog down to the floor. If the rotational force of the pronation exceeds the vertical force of the arm, the arm will be pushed up.

For a simple illustration of this action, make a fist around one end of a long pencil. Place the fist flat on a table, knuckles up. If the forearm is now pronated without using any muscles of the upper arm, the fist and the entire arm will be pushed upward. On the cello, when we make sure that the bow is not being pushed off its track, we are making use of the following principle:

Rotational force and partial arm weight always balance each other.

The capacity of the arm to press down vertically is much greater than the force available for the moment of rotation. With no muscles pressing down actively, the weight of the arm alone by far outweighs the available balancing rotational force at the tip of the bow. Therefore we need to concentrate on pronation in situations where considerable effort is required to achieve a balance with the arm weight—for the production of loud tones at the tip of the bow. Since the arm has strong lifting muscles we need not concern ourselves with them, but we must remember that each pronation reduces the weight of the upper arm by the amount of force that presses on the string.

Another important matter is the rotational force, which changes not only with the variation in the weight of the arm but also with the distance between the hand and the string. This well-known fact can be explained by the law of levers, but the explanation does not quite account for the pressure relationships. The law of levers would explain matters adequately if the bow telescoped into itself or if it had no weight of its own. But as the frog approaches the string in an up bow, the weight of the bow hanging on the other side of the string increases at the same rate and creates a leverage that strengthens the pressure of the bow.

Here is another simple experiment: Hold the bow with two fingers at the screw of the frog and put the tip on a letter scale. A bow usually weighs about 80 grams (3 ounces), and if its weight were distributed evenly along its length, the scale would read 40 grams. But since the bow is heavier at the frog than at the tip, the scale will read only about 30 grams, the rest being supported by the hand. If the frog is slowly moved closer to the scale in an up-bow motion, the scale will show a gradual increase in weight. Remember that this experiment involves no rotational force. Now lead the bow to its balance point. If you let go of it now, it will remain balanced on the scale, and the scale will show its entire weight. If you go beyond this point, the screw must be pressed down with the fingers to keep the bow from tipping over to the other side. This will make the weight on the scale increase beyond 80 grams. Close to the frog you will have to press so hard that the resulting weight will be greater than what is required in actual playing.

Such a crescendo between the tip and the frog is scarcely ever needed. Therefore try to keep the weight on the scale constant while pushing the bow across it in an up-bow motion. Now hold the bow again with two fingers and put it down on the scale at any point. The partial weight of the bow now shown by the scale is called the *effective weight of the bow*.* Now assume a normal bow grip with the hand and play a down bow starting at this point. In order to achieve an even weight on the scale, the rotational force of the pronation must increase continually until it has reached its maximum at the tip. Go back to the starting point (where the rotational force is zero) and play an up bow. In order to keep the weight the same the moment of rotation must be negative; that is, the rotational force becomes a forearm rotation in the opposite direction (supination). This negative rotational force is highest at the frog. Thus, above the point where no rotational force is applied, even pressure on the string is maintained by pronation, below it by supination.

If the chosen point is close to the tip there will be less weight during the entire course of the bow than if the point is close to the frog. Put another way:

> For each level of pressure, that is, for each dynamic level, there is a point on the bow for which no rotational force is necessary.†

In the experiment with the two fingers (in which the bow is moved from tip to frog without rotational force) the bow passes through all those characteristic points.

---

* Above the balance point this weight is less than the absolute weight of the bow (80 grams) , the rest being supported by the arm; for a point below the balance point the weight is greater than the absolute weight of the bow. The additional weight results from the vertical pressure of the arm (partial arm weight).

† If the pressure is to be less than that of the two fingers without rotational force at the tip, a negative moment of rotation will prevail during the entire course of the bow.

This fact is of some consequence. It is not sufficient to mention only the balance point as a characteristic point of the bow. From the previous discussion we know that this point is only one of a continuous series of points without rotational force. It is the point at which the actual weight of the bow equals the pressure. There is no reason to distinguish it from other points in the series, for that may only lead to erroneous ideas, as for instance, "the pressure must be maintained by pronation past the balance point." This misconception may result in tensions because we will do something different from what we think we are doing. We can scarcely help obeying these laws in trying to play a sound of even volume; if we believe that we must use pronation at a point where supination should have already taken over we will activate the wrong muscles —with familiar consequences.

In an example discussed in the previous chapter, in a broad off-the-string bowing between the frog and balance point, in which the bow leaves the string for a moment after each tone, it is important to know that *no* pronation is needed. The pressure comes straight down from above, and the bowing is close to the point that requires no rotational force.

Pressure Relationships in the Bow Hand

So far we have described the moment of rotation in the pronating or supinating forearm in general terms. Now let us examine how it affects the pressure relationships within the hand.

A discussion of whether the right index finger or the pronation of the forearm transmits the pressure to the bow should be superfluous: The pronation makes only as much power available as the stiff index finger (with activated muscles) can manage to transmit to the bow stick. This equilibrium is similar to the one between arm pressure and the moment of rotation. If the index finger were to press by itself (which is hard to imagine physically), the forearm would roll over in the direction of supination; if the pronation alone were to press, the index finger would collapse. Therefore we may state:

The force of the index finger and of the pronation balance each other.

One often hears that "the thumb and the middle finger form a rotational axis." We could conceivably construct such an axis by lifting index finger, ring finger, and little finger off the bow and by rotating the hand around the "axis" formed by the middle finger and the thumb, but that does not correspond to what really happens. If all the fingers are put down on the bow and the hand is pronated slightly, *all* the fingers will rotate, each around the axis situated at its own point of contact with the bow stick.

It is important, however, to avoid an exaggerated rotational movement of the hand toward the bow stick. On the contrary, in order to transmit the rotational force the index finger needs to be stiffened. The visible movement that results is a side effect of the flexibility of the fingers. The smaller this movement the faster the stiffening of the index finger and the faster the pressure is transmitted to the stick.

A simple experiment refutes the notion of the rotational axis: One can play with ease even if the middle finger is taken off the bow stick. Even if both the middle and the ring finger are taken off the bow stick it is possible to play at all dynamic levels, although not comfortably. It seems more meaningful to look at the activity of each individual finger in relation to its purpose, namely, to transmit the rotational force to the bow stick by means of alternate stiffening.

Pick up the bow in a normal playing position and hold the tip with the left hand. The first consideration is to hold it in such a way that it does not drop. That is taken care of by the counterpressure of the thumb against the other fingers; this pressure must be great enough that the static friction between the fingers and the wood will be sufficient to hold the bow. It constitutes another equilibrium of forces, this time between the thumb and the other fingers. Merely to hold the bow, the thumb must press as strongly as all the other fingers combined.*

Now remove the left hand from the tip of the bow. So far the bow has been held up with the least effort. If it is not to drop down at the tip, the little finger must press the stick down. At the same time the pressure of the thumb will increase, along with that of all the other fingers. The fingers opposite the thumb must provide enough pressure so that the thumb can maintain its position at the curve of the frog. It is only in this position that the thumb is able to exert the upward pressure necessary for supination and especially for pronation; if it does not penetrate the curve of the frog, the bow stick will slide off when pressure is exerted. It is important to recognize that the index finger can lift up the bow a little with the help of the increased static friction. We can prove this by letting the index finger go; the tip of the bow will fall down.

We can now formulate this important statement:

Supination is transmitted by the vertical pressure of the little finger and by the upward pull of the index finger and the thumb; the pressure against the frog provides the necessary static friction to stabilize the position of the fingers and the thumb hold in the curve of the frog.

Once again hold the tip of the bow with the left hand and create a moment of rotation by pronating and stiffening the index finger, that is, by pressing the tip of the bow down. The index

---

* This situation is slightly simplified. In reality, the tip of the thumb penetrates about 2 millimeters into the curve of the frog. If it penetrated further, the thumb would support the bow without the help of the other fingers, a position that would be impractical.

FIGURE 38

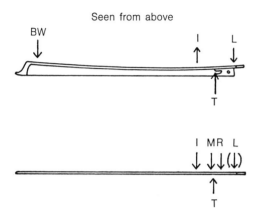

BW: Bow weight, I: Index finger,
L: Little finger, T: Thumb, M: Middle finger,
R: Ring finger

finger presses down, the thumb up. At the same time the pressure of the four fingers against the thumb increases. But something else happens: Even as the index finger pulls the bow up in supination, the little finger now pulls upward with the help of static friction and supports the moment of rotation. This effect can easily be proved by placing the tip of the bow on a letter scale. If the little finger is removed the weight on the scale will diminish. But this help is only possible if the little finger is placed firmly on the ebony of the frog; if the little finger rests on top of the bow stick this is, of course, impossible.

The change in the pressure relationships within the hand during a single stroke of the bow can now be traced easily. At the point described above at which the rotational force changes, the

FIGURE 39

Seen from above

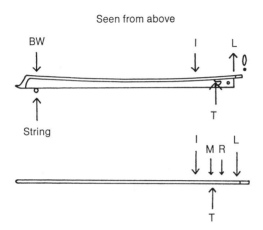

fingers use only as much pressure as they need to hold the bow. If for a loud sound this point is at the frog, all the fingers press down evenly; none press individually. The pressure of the thumb is minimal; its function is to hold the bow. As the bow is moved toward the tip in a down bow, the downward pressure of the index finger and the upward pressure of the thumb increase (along with the upward pull of the little finger). The index finger must exert the most energy because:

> The downward-directed forces (the weight of the bow and the index finger) are as great as the upward-directed forces (the resistance of the string, the thumb, and possibly the little finger) (see Fig. 40).

To simplify matters, let us ignore the activity of the little finger and express this relationship in the following ways:

$$BW + I = T + S \text{ or, } S = BW + I - T.$$

FIGURE 40

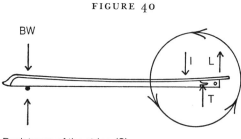

Resistance of the string (S)

The second equation shows that the pressure on the string is as great as the pressure of the index finger plus the weight of the bow minus the pressure of the thumb. We can also say:

$$I = T + S - BW,$$

which means that the pressure of the index finger in pronation is greater than that of the thumb. It increases in proportion to the pressure of the thumb plus the *effective* weight of the bow on the string.

Let us now consider an up bow that starts from the point at which there is no rotational force and approaches the frog. Again the forces directed downward equal those directed upward (see Fig. 41).

$$BW + \overset{\bullet}{L} = S + T + I \text{ or, } S = BW + L - T - I.$$

The second equation shows that in supination the pressure on the string equals that of the little finger plus the weight of the bow minus the upward pull of the index finger and the thumb. It also shows that the little finger has to exert the most energy in supination. Playing pianissimo at the frog for an extended period will cause pain in the little finger. The pressure of the little finger increases in proportion to the combined pull of the thumb and

FIGURE 41

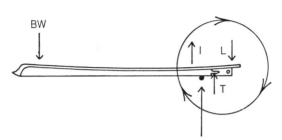

Resistance of the string (S)

the index finger. Fortunately, this pressure never becomes excessive because at a certain point it will cause the bow to leave the
string completely.

It is now clear that it is possible to explain the workings of
the bow hand without mentioning a rotational axis between the
middle finger and the thumb. We can also make one further de-
duction: The pressure of the thumb against the rest of the fingers
need only be enough to keep the thumb from being forced out of
its position by the vertical pressure of either the index finger or
the little finger. More pressure is not only unnecessary (since the
pressure of the thumb and the pressure of the fingers cancel each
other) but may even prevent small pressure impulses from getting
to the string because of the resulting increase in tension. The feel
for the string might also be lost.

The ring finger and the middle finger have no individual
pressure functions, but the ring finger has the task of stabilizing
the tilt of the bow (see below). If this support is missing, the bow
will collapse with each attack and as a result the pressure impulses
of the index finger will be distorted. In this respect the ring finger
performs an important function in the attack.

Holding the Bow

From our investigations of the pressure relationships in the hand we saw that the index finger must transmit most of the rotational force of the pronation. We must therefore find a position in which it can perform its task most easily.

Pick up the bow in a playing position and put the tip on a letter scale. It may seem reasonable to spread the index finger as far as possible in order to achieve the best pressure conditions. For, according to the law of levers, the closer to the tip the pressure is exerted the less finger strength is necessary to transmit a certain amount of pressure to the scale.

Put the index finger down close to the middle finger, opposite the thumb, and try to press firmly on the scale. Then gradually spread the index finger while trying to maintain the same amount of pressure on the bow stick. The increased spread of the finger will increase the pressure on the scale even though the pressure exerted does not increase. Beyond a certain angle of spreading between the index and the middle fingers, this effect will disappear. Since the index finger becomes "longer," its own lever becomes less efficient, and what is gained in energy for the bow is lost in energy for the finger. In addition, the extreme spread of the finger becomes more and more uncomfortable because this position requires considerable muscle activation; moreover, this position increasingly requires the use of the weaker spreading muscles.

There is a degree of spreading at which the greatest possible pressure is achieved with relatively small energy expenditure. It probably occurs when the index finger touches the bow stick at a distance of 5-6 centimeters (2 inches) from the contact point of the thumb. This position would be best for a maximal transmission of pressure at the tip. For relatively little pressure, a more comfortable degree of spread is sufficient, i.e., in soft playing the index finger can be shifted closer to the thumb again.

This does not mean that the angle of the spread between the index finger and the middle finger must change in the course of a single stroke according to the desired dynamic level. That would make the contact of the bow and the string suffer. But we should not entirely renounce the possibility of adjusting to the pressure conditions. There is an opportunity to change the angle slightly, in the bow change at the frog, for instance; no pronation pressure of the index finger is needed here since the bow is already beyond the point where the rotational force changes and the bow arm is already in a supinated position. The index finger should not be too close to the middle finger even in soft playing, for its lifting function is necessary in this position.

The function of the little finger is similar to that of the index finger, but in the opposite sense. In moderately loud playing, its function is limited to the vicinity of the frog, and it may lie close to the ring finger in a relaxed position. In soft playing, it must function as a counterweight during the greater part of the bow stroke so as to transmit the negative moment of rotation; it should therefore be spread a little. In that way the lever that balances the suspended weight of the bow becomes longer and therefore more favorable. If great rotational force is needed to transmit a great deal of pressure at the tip, the little finger may, as described above, strengthen the pressure of the index finger by pulling. For that, it must press against the wood of the frog and it should spread to make good use of the lever effect.

In considering the position of the thumb, the main question is whether the thumb should be flexed or extended in its last joint. If the thumb is strongly flexed, as is often taught, there are several disadvantages. Let us perform this experiment: Rotate the thumb as far as possible with hand stretched out. The main movement will be initiated by the knuckle and the base of the thumb. The last joint will flex when the thumb is moved toward the hand and extend when it is moved away from the hand. Now keep the last joint flexed during the entire circular movement. The movement will be impeded considerably; it is obviously more strenuous to move now.

A further disadvantage is that the flexion also shortens the thumb in the bow grip. The other fingers have to make up for this shortening by flexing more themselves. This would not be a disadvantage if the fingers were all the same length. Try flexing all four fingers together at their middle joints, and imagine a straight line drawn between the middle joints of the index and little fingers. The joints of the middle and ring fingers will stick out past this line. Now take up the bow normally so that the shorter fingers, the index and the little finger, touch the stick with the inside of their last joints. The ring and middle fingers will lose their contact with the stick if they are flexed too much. The fingertips will still touch the lower part of the frog, but in this position they will press the frog toward the thumb, and the tilt of the bow will thus become unstable.

Now hold the bow with the thumb extended so that the inner part of the last joints of middle and ring fingers touch the stick. Try to tilt the bow with the left hand at the tip. The grip of the right hand has to counter this attempt with a certain force. Now flex the thumb (thus making the other fingers flex also). Again try to change the tilt of the bow with the left hand. The same force exerted by the right hand will not be able to resist this tilt, and the bow will fall over.

Thus we see that a grip with an extended thumb makes the two middle fingers stabilize the tilt of the bow by touching the stick as well as the lower part of the frog. In this position the fingers can be kept very flexible in the vertical direction, that is, perpendicular to the palm. The fingers can be extended at the knuckle and flexed at the middle joint; or, conversely, flexed at the knuckle and at the same time extended at the middle joint. The thumb follows this movement by flexing and extending, respectively, at its own knuckle.

A final disadvantage of the strongly flexed position is that the thumb will always touch the frog at the sharp edge. In loud playing at the tip this may become quite painful and therefore cumbersome. If the thumb is slightly extended, the area of contact is greatly expanded. The thumb still touches the edge of the frog, but it also touches part of the ebony at the curve of the frog and, in fact, the bow stick to some extent.

Even so we should not insist that the thumb be totally extended. Since the plane of the flexion of the last joint is parallel to the bow movement, the ability of the thumb to flex in the last joint may be used as an "elastic" element and applied in the bow change.

In the first part of this book we said that a moving joint delivers more exact information to the brain than does an immobile one. Therefore if the last joint of the thumb is allowed to move a little during the bow change, there will be more control than if the thumb were to remain rigid. This means that all fast movements will be technically more secure and looser if the thumb flexes a little in the last joint.

Flexibility in the last joint of the thumb is sometimes desirable even when no bow change is involved. Earlier we discussed the possibility of influencing one side of the body by moving the corresponding joints of the other half of the body. Small movements in the right thumb may sometimes alleviate technical difficulties of the left hand, especially when shifts or trills are involved.

We may summarize the position of the thumb as follows: We must adjust to the changing demands of the instrument with changing positions or movements of the thumb. When great permanent pressure is needed—as in a slow fortissimo—the extended position is preferable. In contrast, fast movements of the bow and of the left hand require greater flexibility in the last joint of the thumb. Starting with a slightly flexed thumb is good preparation.

Another matter that often causes problems is the concept that the bow has to "hang" in the hand. It may mislead a player into flexing the fingers overly at the knuckles and extending them at the middle joint. In addition the wrist will be high. The result is that the index finger must press firmly before it can even start to transmit pressure to the string. Here is an analogy: One can lift a chest by pressing both hands flat against its sides so that the static friction helps lift it, but it is easier to lift it from the lower edge. The mere lifting force is the same in both cases, but in the first considerable effort is necessary even to take hold of the chest. Correspondingly, there is a practical and an impractical position of the index finger.

In Fig. 42a great lateral pressure of the thumb and the other fingers is necessary to produce enough static friction to press the stick down. In Fig. 42b no frictional pressure is necessary; the index finger is in a position where it can press down on the stick without effort. The thumb presses up and needs to exert only enough lateral pressure so that an increase in the pressure of the index finger does not force it out of its position at the curve of the frog.

Slanting the Instrument

So far we have ignored the fact that the cello is not in a horizontal position like the violin but in a slanted position in front of the player because it would have made the explanations too complicated. In general the matters we have dealt with do not change much when the instrument is slanted, but for those who would like to see this factor analyzed more closely, we will enumerate the small changes caused by the slant.

FIGURE 42a

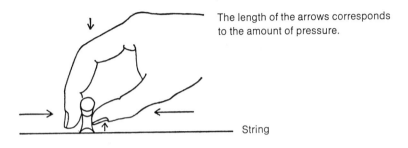

The length of the arrows corresponds
to the amount of pressure.

String

FIGURE 42b

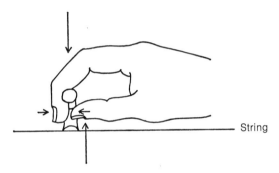

String

To be precise, we cannot speak of the intrinsic weight of the bow resting on the string. This weight would not be directed vertically to the string but vertically to the ground. Let us recall the experiment in which the bow was held with two fingers in order to find out how a single bow stroke operates without rotational force. If this experiment is repeated on a slanted instrument the effective weight of the bow decreases the more upright the instrument is held.

The pressure relationships in the hand, however, do not change when applied to a slanted string rather than to a horizontal one. The observations about the position of the fingers and the rotational force of the forearm pronation are the same. We only need to investigate the question of the weight of the arm in relation to the slanted position.

If the arm is allowed to drop it will not fall toward the ground but toward the body. This means that the direction of its fall corresponds to the direction of its pressure. All points of the extended arm, forearm and hand included, press in a direction perpendicular to the position of the arm at the time and not in a direction perpendicular to the ground, if all muscles are relaxed. The arm may be compared to a pendulum (see Fig. 43).

FIGURE 43

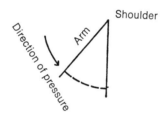

If the bow is put down on the A or the D string in a normal position, the pendulum of the arm does not push in a direction perpendicular to the ground but perpendicular to the string. If the arm is moved to the middle of the bow, the direction of the pressure of the pendulum on the string does not change because the arm would fall toward the body if all the muscles relaxed. As the bow continues to move, the arm takes a diagonal position in front of the body. If it were allowed to drop it would fall toward the body, i.e., the direction of its force is diagonal to the body.

This pressure can be understood as the combination of two kinds of pressure:

1. the pressure perpendicular to the string, and
2. the pressure in the direction of the tip (of the up bow).

We are dealing with a parallelogram of forces (see Fig. 44) whose components are the force perpendicular to the string and the force in the direction of the up bow. The result is the force

FIGURE 44

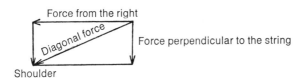

Force from the right

Diagonal force

Force perpendicular to the string

Shoulder

active in a direction diagonal to the body. The energy that must be provided by the arm muscles in order to keep the arm up therefore opposes these forces. A parallelogram of the opposing forces would look like Fig. 45.

FIGURE 45

Muscle activity away from the string (S)

Muscle activity diagonally to the right

Muscle activity to the right (r)

Shoulder

Force S may be replaced partially or altogether by the pressure of the string against the bow; in that case the muscles need not work in the direction of *S,* but must only keep the arm up in the direction of force *r.* It follows that:

> The weight of the arm borne by the muscles is reduced by the amount of force applied perpendicularly to the string, which is transmitted to the string as pressure.

This statement corresponds to our former examinations of the arm weight.

On the lower strings the force pressing perpendicularly hardly changes; it still holds true that the pressure on the string reduces the arm weight. The greater this pressure is the less is the force that must support the arm.

On the lower strings only the direction of the horizontal force changes (the force active in the direction of the bow track). For instance on the C string, this force operates in the direction of the down bow (on the A string in the direction of the up bow). To play the sequence of notes in Fig. 46 the arm must be lifted continuously for up bow and down bow.

FIGURE 46

Thus we see that slanting the instrument does not change anything of importance in the original observations, based on the cello in an assumed horizontal position.

X

MOVEMENT OF
THE RIGHT ARM

Upper Arm and Forearm in a Whole-Bow Stroke

LET US proceed in the familiar way and ask first of all which movements our instrument requires for a whole-bow stroke. We need not explain in detail why the ideal movement of the bow must form a right angle with the string. If that is not the case, part of the pulling power of the bow, which makes the string vibrate by means of static friction, is lost (see Fig. 47). This lost energy also disturbs the formation of the amplitude and we hear ugly side noises.

FIGURE 47

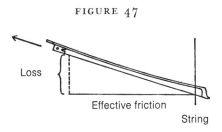

The only effective friction is the component running perpendicularly to the string; the friction of the other component, the loss, operates parallel to the string and disturbs the vibrations of the string. Friction that runs parallel to the string expands the length of the string but does not support the lateral static friction. (Small deviations, however, will barely be noticeable.)

We can also construct a case in which the direction of the bow movement runs perpendicular to the string but the bow itself approaches from an oblique angle. In this case no friction is lost

FIGURE 48

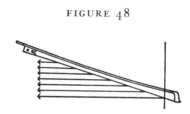

since at each point the bow pulls in a direction perpendicular to the string; the rapid change of contact place, however, which in this case occurs during a single stroke, changes all the conditions of sound production.

In the second case, the noise of the friction increases only when the bow forms an extremely acute angle with the string, an angle that even beginners never use. It seems to be somewhat paradoxical that a stroke that stays at the same point of the string and uses a slanted direction may disturb and even destroy the vibrations much more than does a stroke that glides along the string. Therefore to change contact points without affecting the sound we may use a slanted bow moving in a direction perpendicular to the string.

If, however, we wish the bow to touch the same point on the

string during the entire stroke, the track and the position of the bow must coincide, i.e., the bow track must form a right angle with the string. The arm therefore must lead the bow hand from frog to tip along a straight line, perpendicular to the string. However, the body cannot describe a straight line by using only one joint. Each limb describes an arc of a circle by flexing and extending at its joint.

Describing a straight line always requires the participation of several joints. This fact is important to note, since we often hear that the lower part of the bow stroke is executed by the upper arm and the upper part by the forearm. It is mechanically impossible to do this. At each point of the bow stroke the forearm and the upper arm function together, or, more clearly: There is no point at which the movement is executed by just the shoulder or by just the elbow.

The following discussion concerns the upper arm and the forearm but not the hand and the fingers. Let us see how the end point of the forearm (the wrist) describes a straight line: The track of the wrist runs parallel to the track of the bow. Consider the shoulder as the steady pivot point of the upper arm. The distance between it and the track of the wrist changes continually as the wrist moves. This distance can only be changed if the elbow is flexed to various degrees; if the elbow maintained the same angle for any length of time, the track of the wrist would be circular instead of straight. Fig. 49 is a simplified presentation of these facts on a plane; in three-dimensional space the elbow would be behind the plane of the drawing. That does not change the relationship of the angles, however.

Let us select four characteristic positions of the arm:

1. at the frog
2. at the balance point of the bow (the distance between the shoulder and the wrist is shortest at this point)

FIGURE 49

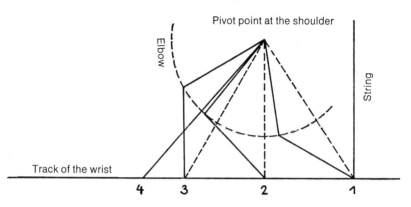

3. in the upper third of the bow (the bow and the forearm form a right angle)

4. at the tip (with the arm extended)

From Fig. 49 we can deduce that:

1. The elbow is more extended in position *1* than in position *2*, since the distance between the shoulder and the hand is greater.

2. In position *2* the shoulder-hand connection forms a right angle with the track of the wrist. The distance between the shoulder and the wrist is the shortest, and therefore the angle at the elbow is the most acute.

3. In position *3* the angle at the elbow is about the same as in position *1*.

4. In position *3* the elbow reaches its highest point.

5. In position *4* the angle at the elbow is the most obtuse.

6. In position *4* the elbow is lower (in three-dimensional space further forward) than in position *3*.

In the lower half of the bow the participation of the upper arm prevails, while in the upper half the elbow extends increasingly. From the drawing we can see, however, that it is wrong to attribute part of the bow stroke solely to the upper arm or solely to the forearm.

It is interesting to note that the upper arm reverses its direction for a short stretch on the same bow (between position *3* and position *4*). It is also important that in the up bow the angle of the elbow again becomes more obtuse near the frog—the same change of angle as at the tip in a down bow.

Trying to separate the movements of the upper arm and the forearm according to Fig. 49 points up how useless such a separation is even for teaching a beginner. Fig. 50 shows that the resulting two arcs of a circle describing the tracks of the wrist and of the bow do not fulfil the demands of our instrument.

FIGURE 50

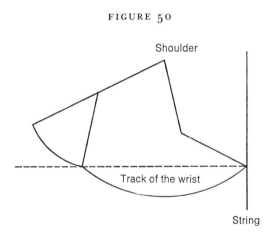

Let us now isolate position *3* of Fig. 49. If we assume that the angle at the elbow is constant we may rotate the arm around the axis *S–H* behind and in front of the plane of Fig. 51. This drawing must be seen in space. With the angle at the elbow held constant, the position of the elbow changes, but the distance between the

FIGURE 51

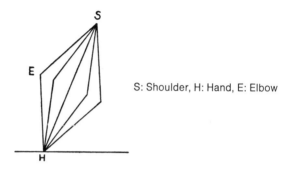

S: Shoulder, H: Hand, E: Elbow

shoulder and the wrist does not. The elbow and the entire arm may be held high or low without affecting the track of the bow. This leeway in the elbow will be important for string changes. (We have already encountered it when we examined the equilibrium of the body.)

We often hear that holding the elbow as low as possible will help the "arm weight." There is no position of the elbow that is always "right." Such a position would only be possible if we were to use the same amount of pressure and did not move the body at all. Instead we must say:

> The elbow must be as low as is comfortable and as high as necessary for a particular pressure.

Two considerations may be used to prove this statement:

1. The static energy of a pendulum is greater the closer it approaches its horizontal position. If the upper arm is held in a horizontal position with the forearm hanging down, the musculature of the upper arm must actively support this "high pendulum." The lower the upper arm, that is, the lower the elbow, the less energy is necessary to hold it. At the same time there is an increase

in the energy that the biceps must provide to maintain the angle at the elbow. Since the forearm weighs less than the entire arm, less energy is necessary at a low-elbow position than at a high one.

2. Pronation must create the rotational force that transmits the weight of the arm to the string. If the elbow is kept low, the palm normally opens to the left. To hold the bow properly, the palm must be at least horizontal. The hand can manage to assume a horizontal position even with a low elbow if the forearm is pronated; but no further possibility of rotation remains to transmit additional pressure to the string, for the pronation has already reached its limit.

If the upper arm is allowed to hang and form an angle with the forearm while the palm opens to the left, and then the elbow is lifted, the palm will be turned down, as much as an angle of 90 degrees. At this point the upper arm will be horizontal. From this position the hand can still be turned another 90 degrees, this time with the help of actual pronation, since the forearm starts from a position in the middle between extreme pronation and extreme supination. This additional leeway for pronation is not needed as a movement, of course, but it increases the pressure reserve considerably. This we can prove with another experiment using a letter scale:

Take up the bow and put the tip on the scale. Now press on the scale as hard as possible, once with a low elbow, once with a high elbow. With the elbow low the scale will register about half what it will with the elbow high. Thus we can deduce:

An increase in dynamics requires an appropriately higher elbow position.

Of course, at the other extreme, it would be foolish to try to play with a high elbow and thus increase the strain of supporting the weight of the arm if little or no pronation pressure is necessary; for instance, near the frog, where pronation is needed only for extreme pressure. At the frog the elbow should therefore be brought close to the body.

We can now dispense with such concepts as "a low arm is heavier" or that we should "play with the whole arm." There is more than enough arm weight available in any situation. Thus, an advisable substitution for the recommendation "play with the whole arm" may be "use more bow."

One final warning: So far we have assumed that the shoulder is a pivot point that is steady, whereas in fact it can make rather big circular movements. It can be pushed forward, up, and back. If the shoulder is habitually raised, unnecessary muscle activity will result, which may hinder the control of small motor impulses in the entire right arm. A raised shoulder is also a visual expression of insecurity and should be avoided.

Hand and Finger Movements during a Whole-Bow Stroke

If in Fig. 49 the hand is added as an extension of the forearm, the bow will point into the air at the frog and hang down at the tip, as in Fig. 52. We need a mechanism that can change the angle formed by forearm and the bow so that the bow will form a right angle with the string at every position of the arm. That mechanism is the wrist, which can change the lateral angle formed by the hand and the forearm. Flexing the right hand at the wrist to the left, i.e., toward the body, is *adduction;* flexing it to the right, i.e., away from the body, is *abduction.* In the ideal case the hand would need to *abduct* only at the frog and *adduct* only at the tip. Fig. 53 is a two-dimensional simplification of this mechanism.

The ability of the hand to adduct and abduct is, however, limited. Since the required angles are too great to be reached in this way, other ways of compensating are needed. For the position at the frog we can make use of the fact that the bow is normally not perpendicular to the axis of the hand. If the bow stick is placed

FIGURE 52

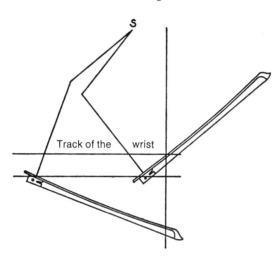

in the last joints of the index and little fingers, the axis of the hand does not form a right angle but an obtuse angle with the bow

FIGURE 53

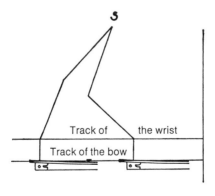

FIGURE 54

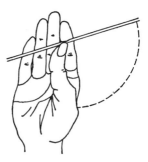

since the index finger is longer than the little finger (Fig. 54). Because of that the hand forms a slightly oblique angle with the track of the bow at the frog, and, by means of the angle of abduction, achieves the necessary compensation (Fig. 55).

FIGURE 55

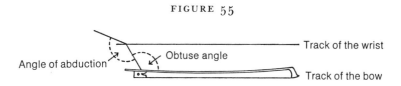

Since the elbow is lower at the frog than at the tip, the wrist is flexed volarly at the frog (i.e., in a direction perpendicular to the palm) so that the wrist comes up. Side views in Fig. 56 show the difference between the angle of the wrist at the tip and at the frog.

The position of the hand itself (i.e., the angle formed by the axis of the hand and the ground) has not changed. The obtuse angle formed by the bow and the hand (Fig. 54) has one disadvan-

FIGURE 56

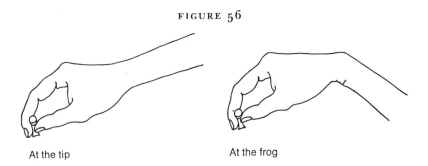

At the tip   At the frog

tage for the position at the tip: The hand must be adducted even further to compensate for it. See Fig. 57. This angle cannot be

FIGURE 57

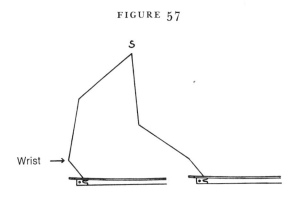

formed by adduction of the hand alone. However, it can be changed by flexing the index finger and extending the little finger, as in Fig. 58.

We thus possess a means of varying the angle formed by the bow and the hand. Flexing the index finger in this case means flexing at the middle joint and extending at the knuckle. The in-

FIGURE 58

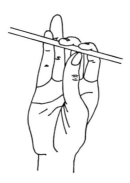

dex finger is flexed more at the tip than at the frog. The little finger is flexed more at the frog than at the tip. The flexion of the index finger at the tip together with the extension of the little finger implies at the same time a pronating movement; or, expressed better, near the tip of the bow, the fingers yield to a pronating movement.

A common error in string technique is to confuse the pronating *movement* with pronation *pressure*. One, however, precludes the other: If the index finger yields to a pronating movement by flexing (and by extending at the knuckle), *no* pronation pressure results. Only when it stiffens and does *not* yield, so that no movement becomes visible, can the pronation pressure be transmitted to the bow stick. Thus the pressure on the string is independent of the pronating position; even if an up bow is played in the air without putting the bow on the string this pronating movement can be discerned.

In the course of one bow, changes in the pronation pressure and the pronating movement occur simultaneously. The pronation pressure increases in the down bow together with a stiffening of the index finger, while *in addition,* the hand pronates. The degree of the pronation position does not indicate the degree of pronation *pressure*. (Of course, if the index finger is stiffened in advance and then a fast pronation movement is made the pronation pressure will increase in accordance with this movement.)

The degree of pronation must change between the frog and the tip in order to compensate for the changing angle formed by the hand and the bow. Since the forearm is pronated more at the tip, we make use of the dorsal flexibility of the hand at the wrist (in the direction of the back of the hand) and change the angle if necessary to find a comfortable position. A short arm will need this kind of compensation more than a long one, since in a short arm the elbow must be extended further to reach the tip. This will in turn make the angle formed by forearm and bow more acute (Fig. 59).

FIGURE 59

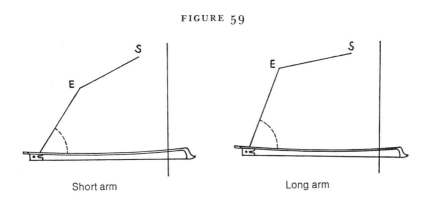

Short arm   Long arm

The dorsal position should not be used more than is abso lutely necessary, for a strong break at the wrist is impractical for the transmission of pressure. The fact that the bow would be tilted excessively would not be bad in itself, but maintaining the original direction of the pressure of the index finger would push the bow toward the bridge. To avoid that the index finger would have to be flexed at the middle joint, too; it would, so to speak, pull the bow onto the string (Fig. 60a) instead of pressing it down from above (Fig. 60b).

FIGURE 60

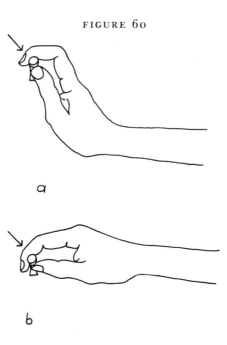

a

b

Let us summarize: At the frog, the bow and the forearm form an obtuse angle; at the tip they form an acute angle. To achieve the necessary angles we must keep the following in mind:

1. At the frog the bow and the hand form an obtuse angle.

2. At the frog this oblique position of the hand together with a slight abduction achieve the necessary set of angles.

3. At the frog the wrist is a little high, i.e., the hand is in a volar position.

4. In the course of a down bow, the forearm increasingly pronates.

5. Toward the tip, the index finger flexes while the little finger extends; this in part makes possible the necessary acute angle.

6. At the tip the hand is in an adducted position.

7. A slightly dorsal position of the hand can achieve a more acute angle between the bow and the pronated forearm.

Bow Change

We have seen that the initiation of a sound has an important technical as well as musical function, for the attack characterizes the sound and thus the entire playing. The articulation and clarity of the musical interpretation are determined by the attack.

We can also look at the bow change as the initiation of a sound. The problems of the attack and those of the bow change are therefore related. The oft-heard demand that the bow change be "inaudible" is impossible to fulfil. But what is meant by this desirable inaudibility? Just as there are two possible ways of attacking a sound, so are there two ways of changing bows:

1. The string may gradually be brought up to full amplitude on the new bow. This means that at the beginning of the new bow the pressure and the speed must increase. The natural pendulum characteristics of the arm can be used, and compensating movements of the hand and the fingers reduced to a minimum. The conditions are similar to those of the soft attack.

2. The sound may be sustained at its full volume, i.e., the bow may approach the change at full speed and full pressure. The change of the bow itself has to be abrupt and the new tone must reach its full amplitude right away. The arm alone cannot manage such an abrupt movement; the hand and the fingers must support the arm movement.

Both kinds of bow changes can be called inaudible in a certain sense:

1. In the first type the plosive noise of the attack can be avoided. Instead there will be a break in volume, since we cannot achieve a crescendo at the beginning of the new tone without making a slight diminuendo at the end of the previous bow.

2. In the second, the break in volume can be avoided. It is virtually uninterrupted during the change. But the price of this continuity is a more or less hard plosive noise, although it is not as hard in a bow change as at the beginning of a tone after a rest. In the latter case the ear perceives the plosive sound as the beginning of the full volume; in the bow change, the ear registers only the difference in loudness between the previous tone and the plosive sound itself. In the second kind of bow change, even a relatively strong plosive noise will not give the impression of a disturbing accent, but only that of a welcome articulation within a very tight sound.

Needless to say, both kinds may be used as artistic means of expression. The soft bow change, with its diminuendo at the end of the previous bow and crescendo at the beginning of the new bow, seems gentle and restrained in its expression. For intensive playing, however, we need the second kind; even lyrical passages can be very "tight" and intensive.

We have already dealt with the technical execution of the soft bow change in connection with the soft attack; the increase in pressure and the increase in speed must correspond to each other. The execution of the "tight" change, however, must be examined a bit more closely.

For this kind of change the vibrating string demands that the bow maintain its full pressure and speed until the end of the bow. It is stopped abruptly at the moment of the change and must turn around without delay and at once resume its full speed. If the arm were to execute this abrupt change of direction by itself, great force of muscle would have to be activated at the moment of the change to slow down and then resume the speed so suddenly.

Try to change as tightly as possible with the hand and the fingers completely stiff. This is possible to a certain degree, easier at the tip than at the frog. The whole body is shaken by the impact of this sudden effort. In a short time the body is completely tense because continuous muscle effort is necessary to counter these impacts and maintain the equilibrium of the body. The hand and the wrist must also be activated so that they are not tossed further according to the laws of inertia.

This tightness can be avoided by using the familiar pendulum movement of the arm, by slowing down the arm at the end of the previous bow and accelerating it at the beginning of the new bow. To the extent to which the arm decreases its speed, the movement of the hand and the fingers must take over. Not only is this necessary for maintaining the speed until the end of the previous sound but also it corresponds to the natural laws of inertia. The hand and fingers keep moving in the same direction because of the motor energy provided by the whole arm.

At the frog, i.e., for the change from up bow to down bow, while the arm slows down, the hand and fingers start their own acceleration. The speed of the bow remains constant. Finally, the arm movement stops altogether, while the hand and fingers maintain their own speed by changing the angle accordingly. The arm now starts its reverse movement, while the hand and fingers are still moving in the previous direction with the original speed. For a short time the arm is moving in the opposite direction to the fingers. By the end of this hand movement the arm has reached its full speed in the new direction. The hand, the fingers, and the bow are at the end of their range of movement and are now pulled along in the opposite direction by the arm, which has resumed full speed. The muscle exertion required for the entire process is no

greater than for the soft bow change. The arm may swing back
and forth as a "pendulum," and the hand and fingers are first
tossed in the old direction and then taken along in the new direction without additional muscle effort.

These phases can be shown by the diagram in Fig. 61, in
which the lengths of the arrows correspond to the speed. (To simplify matters the movement of the fingers has been omitted.) For

FIGURE 61

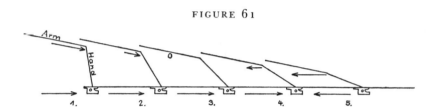

the arm the change from full speed in one direction to full speed
in the opposite direction takes place relatively slowly between
phases *1* and *5;* but for the bow the change is abrupt and occurs
between phases *4* and *5.* Between phases *1* and *5* the angle formed
by the forearm and the hand becomes more and more obtuse (in
a dorsal direction). A compensating lowering of the forearm, that
is, of the wrist, is required to prevent the bow from lifting off the
string (Fig. 62a).

At the same time as the wrist is lowered, it must also be pulled
back a little, since the length of the hand and fingers is the same
in both positions. Fig. 62 shows a side view of this movement.
Without this pulling back, the bow would move closer to the
bridge (Fig. 62b).

There is a situation, however, in which we can use the movement described by Fig. 62b: an ascending shift together with a
bow change at the frog. With care we can reach the new contact
point required by the shortened string inaudibly.

FIGURE 62

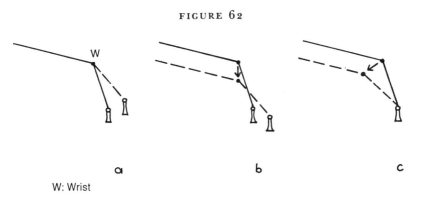

a   b   c

W: Wrist

We have to be careful, however, that the speed of the hand, fingers, and bow is not greater than the previous speed of the entire arm. With some string players an acceleration at the end of the previous bow can be observed; it produces an ugly, additional pressure at the end of each tone. The compensating movement of the hand and fingers is meant to complement the diminishing speed of the arm, not to increase the speed of the bow. The compensating movement of the hand and fingers is larger the greater the speed of the arm. It is awkward to make a large motion with the wrist at the end of a long, slow stroke; the contact with the string and the uniformity of the movement and tone would be severely disturbed.

Since the speed of the bow before and after the change between two slow strokes is also slow, the arm can provide most of the necessary decelerating and accelerating energy; the movement of the hand and fingers may be small. If, on the other hand, the momentum of the arm is also small, the braking effect of the friction between the bow and the string becomes more noticeable. The energy of the tossed hand is no longer sufficient; the fingers must participate more actively the slower the speed of the bow.

This does not change the rules of the bow change, however; the wrist must still be lowered and pulled back, but with a smaller movement.

As seen earlier in the discussion of the whole-bow stroke, a change in the angle formed by the forearm and the hand naturally causes a change in the angle formed by the axis of the hand and the bow (Figs. 54 and 58). The mechanism for this process is familiar: The angle formed by the axis of the hand and the bow is changed by the alternate flexion of the index finger and the little finger. In this way the bow remains at right angles to the string throughout the change.

For the bow change at the tip, the principles are the same, but the hand is in a different position and requires a different kind of compensation. At the tip, the hand is in a pronated position. If it were tossed out in the direction of the bow track, in a movement analogous to the one at the frog, a combination of lateral and vertical movements (volar and abducted movements) of the wrist would be necessary. The schematic presentation in Fig. 63 may explain these movements.

The shift of the slanted palm parallel to the bow track has one component in a direction perpendicular to the palm (the volar

FIGURE 63

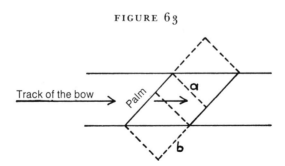

Track of the bow

movement, *a*) and one component in the plane of the palm (the abduction movement, *b*). From above, the abduction movement looks like Fig. 64. It has one disadvantage in that the abduction pushes the contact place of the index finger forward (arrow) and away from the stick; at the very moment when the force of the index finger is most necessary for the resumption of full amplitude, some pressure is lost. This loss may be compensated for quickly with additional pronation, but the tiny disturbance prevents a tight change at the tip. Since the movement in Fig. 63 includes this abducting movement, it cannot produce an ideal bow change.

FIGURE 64

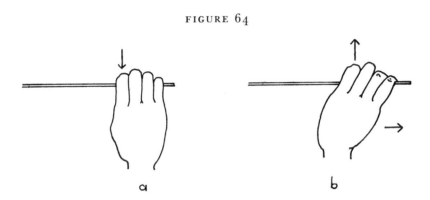

a   b

Let us resort to a special tactic: If we remove the lateral abduction component of Fig. 63, the movement will look like the diagram in Fig. 65. The effective length of the bow stroke is shorter than that in Fig. 63, but the advantage is that we are using a simple volar movement, which is much easier for the hand, instead of a combination of movements. We may ignore the deviation from the bow track.

A decisive advantage has been achieved with respect to the

FIGURE 65

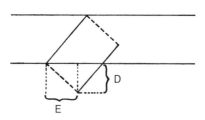

D: Deviation from the bow track,
E: Effective length of the bow stroke

pressure of the index finger. By dispensing with the abduction movement and deviating a little from the bow track, we have made it possible for the index finger to maintain contact with the stick during the entire change. In addition it gains a little pressure by the following means: If the tip of the bow rests on the string and the hand and frog are lowered *without changing the position of the palm in the direction of supination,* the pressure on the stick increases. The downward movement of the hand has the effect of an increase in pressure (pronation, relatively speaking) because the angle formed by the bow and the hand changes (Fig. 66). And this increase can be put to good use at the moment the string starts vibrating again.

FIGURE 66

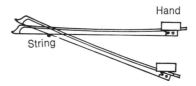

At the tip, we therefore have at our disposal a movement of the wrist (together with a little movement of the fingers in the same direction) that helps the arm to slow down and reaccelerate, and provides the change with a tight contact between the index finger and the bow stick. The bow describes the track shown in Fig. 67.

FIGURE 67

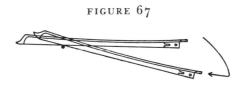

One occasionally hears a recommendation that the bow make a "round" movement during the change at the tip. This advice is certainly based on the feeling that one can make a better bow change with the movement just described, but this process is not accurately described as *round*. A round movement will contribute nothing to a tight bow change at the tip, but will look like Fig. 68. The effective speed is slowed down gradually between

FIGURE 68

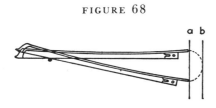

a and *b,* and accelerated gradually between *b* and *a.* Thus there is no reason not to stay on the same track and slow down and accelerate there.

In addition to the movement of the hand, a small finger movement is useful at the tip; this is again analogous to the one at the frog. While at the frog the index finger extends and the little finger flexes, the reverse occurs at the tip: The index finger flexes and the little finger extends. This additional movement is very small, however.

Finally we use another movement more or less automatically. Imagine that the axis of pronation of the forearm is extended past the hand. The hand and the bow will lie below this axis. At the tip, the hand and the bow are closer to this axis; in a dorsal position the axis extends to the contact point of the thumb at the frog. Apart from this position, however, the hand remains below the extension of the axis of pronation during most of the bow stroke.

Let us try another experiment: Hold the right forearm horizontally, with the hand hanging down loosely. Now move the forearm to the left and stop the movement suddenly. The hand will fly farther to the left; at the same time, the forearm will rotate passively around its axis of pronation in the direction of supination. If the hand is moved to the right, the abrupt halt creates a passive pronation movement. When we say that the hand is tossed farther at the bow change because of its weight, we should not forget the implied passive pronation and supination movement.

To make it possible for the hand to be tossed farther in an up bow at the frog, the hand should arrive in a rather pronated position. If the change from down bow to up bow occurs in the middle of the bow, the hand will be tossed farther to the right and the forearm will pronate passively. This means that the following up bow will be in a more pronated position than the previous down bow.

The tossing force of the weight of the hand creates a passive forearm rotation during the change; but there is another force—

the frictional resistance of the bowed string—that influences the rotation of the forearm during the course of the bow. This friction slows down the bow and therefore the hand, so that the hand is forced to "pull the bow behind." The frictional resistance has the effect of supination in the down bow and that of pronation in the up bow. In other words:

At the same place on the bow the hand is more supinated in the down bow than in the up bow.

It would be foolish to try to work actively against the passive pronation and supination movements occurring in the change, since at the next bow change the additional mobility will be welcome.

The closer to the tip the change takes place the smaller the forearm rotation will be. Since the hand must be pronated near the tip anyway, and since the fingers approach the extended axis of the forearm more and more, the change will not result in further pronation. The volar movement in the wrist described above takes over as a complementary movement.

In the course of each up bow the pronation position acquired at the tip is maintained to a certain degree and provides mobility for the compensating movement at the frog. The forearm therefore rotates in the following way during one up bow and down bow:

1. During the up bow the arm keeps a pronated position.
2. For the change at the frog the arm supinates somewhat.
3. During the down bow the arm increasingly pronates.
4. For the change at the tip, the arm hardly pronates. A change from down bow to up bow in the middle or lower part of the bow results in a clearly visible pronation movement.

Thus with regard to forearm motion, the up bow is not an exact reversal of the down bow.

We saw in Fig. 61 that the wrist has a higher position at the frog before the change than after. Since there is no reason for actively changing the position of the wrist after the bow change, it is lower during the down bow than during the up bow. Since the hand is more pronated during the up bow than the down, the degree of flexion of the index and little fingers changes. During the up bow the index finger is flexed more and the little finger extended more than during the down bow.

Let us now summarize all the conditions that are important for the bow change:

1. The most comfortable movement of the arm is that of the pendulum, which consists of acceleration at the beginning and deceleration at the end of the movement. This course of movement, together with the necessary decrease and increase in pressure, would result in a diminuendo on the previous tone and a crescendo on the next tone.

2. While the arm slows down, the hand and fingers finish the movement; for one short moment the arm and the bow move in opposite directions.

3. In the bow change the angle at the wrist changes. In order to maintain a right angle between the bow and the string, the hand must change its angle to the bow. It does so by alternating flexing the index finger and extending the little finger with flexing the little finger and extending the index finger.

4. The up bow differs from the down bow in that
    a. the forearm pronates more
    b. the index finger is flexed more and the little finger is extended more
    c. the wrist is in a higher position.

5. At the frog, the widening of the angle at the wrist is compensated for by a lowering and pulling back of the wrist.

6. At the tip, the movement perpendicular to the palm (volar

movement) compensates for the change; a small deviation from the original bow track provides additional pressure at the moment of the change.

String Change

The bow tracks of the two neighboring strings lie at a particular angle to each other (see Fig. 69). The greater the distance from the vertex of that angle the greater is the distance between the two sides. The distance the hand must travel to change from one string to the next is several times greater at the tip (distance *a*) than at the frog (distance *b*).

FIGURE 69

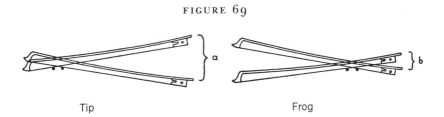

Tip   Frog

In addition, independent of the distance between the hand and the vertex (that is, the string), the degree of pronation of the hand with respect to the bow must be the same on both strings in order to guarantee the same pressure on both bow paths. Therefore the pronation positions for two neighboring strings form the same angle as that formed by the two bow tracks, no matter whether we are playing at the frog or at the tip. We must therefore find a movement that leads the bow from one string to another comfortably at the various distances between the frog and the string. In addition, the pronation of the hand must adjust to the change in the angle between the bow tracks.

Let us start with the upper part of the bow, where the hand

must travel the farthest (see Fig. 70). To transfer the entire arm to the new bow path at the moment of the change would require considerable effort. Not only would this movement strongly shake the body and disturb the contact between the bow and the string but it would also be disadvantageous for the left hand. There are three ways of distributing the arm movement over a longer period of time, so that the arm approaches the new bow track gradually:

1. The arm may approach the new track in an even movement. At the moment of the rhythmically intended change the bow touches the new string.

2. The upper arm (that is, the elbow) may be lifted or lowered before the change into the position that the new bow track requires. Fig. 51 shows how the elbow may change its position without a movement in the hand. At the moment of the change only the forearm and hand have to follow.

3. The elbow may be lifted or lowered beyond the new position. At the moment of the actual change the forearm rotates around a point approximately in its middle, so that the hand moves into the new path while the elbow pulls back a little.

All three ways are possible. Let us consider their advantages and disadvantages:

1. The first movement is only possible if it is executed very slowly. The bow must touch the next string at the rhythmically exact moment. This moment, however, is not marked by a rhythmical impulse in the body; the movement is begun earlier and the moment when the new string is touched depends on the speed of the movement and the distance between the two bow tracks. During the playing this distance varies, and a degree of rhythmic imprecision is the result. That might be corrected by a small jolt shortly before the new string is touched, but that would again

FIGURE 70

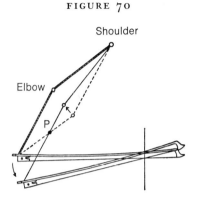

P: Pivot point of the forearm

Initial position

Intermediate position

Final position

shake the entire arm, which is what we are trying to avoid. The first way is therefore not appropriate for a rhythmically precise bow change, if we want to prevent the body from shaking.

2. If the elbow is brought into the new position before the actual (audible) change much less energy is needed for pulling the forearm into the new position at the moment of the change. That is done with a rotation of the upper arm. The rhythmic impulse for this final phase of the total movement occurs shortly before the actual string change; the beginning of the new tone can be controlled better rhythmically than with the first way. If this second type is executed very quickly, however, there will still be a certain amount of shaking, which will be transmitted through the arm, but for a slow bow change this way is entirely satisfactory.

3. The third way looks a little confusing at first. One might ask why move the elbow beyond the new position and then back again. We need to digress a little to explain this.

Pick up a long object, for instance, the bow, at one end, using two fingers. Let the other end hang to the ground. Then move the upper end back and forth. The lower end will not move parallel to the upper one. The mass inertia of the object makes the hanging part stay behind the part that is actively moved; in a fast back-and-forth movement a pivot point is formed somewhere below the middle. The hanging end moves in exactly the opposite direction to the actively moved part. This means that, relatively speaking, this kind of movement requires the least effort.

A counter experiment will prove that: Hold the object firmly in the fist in order to force the lower end to move parallel to the upper one. This action requires much more effort than the previous one.

In yet another experiment, the fist holds the object without moving back and forth, but makes the lower end move by turning the upper end back and forth. This effort is less than that needed for the previous experiment but still much more than for the first one.

A seesaw is a good example: Only a little effort is required to keep it going, but if it were broken off at the pivot point much more energy would be needed to move the remaining side in the same way. Around this pivot point a kind of double level is created, with the energy produced on one side of it balancing the energy on the other side. We can thus formulate the following statement:

> If a long object is to be moved back and forth at one end, a minimum amount of effort will be needed if the other end

is moved in the opposite direction so that a pivot point is formed in the middle.

We find the same conditions in the arm: To move the end of a long object, that is, the end of the forearm, the least amount of effort will be expended if the other end of the object, the elbow, is moved in the opposite direction. The energy for this movement will be furnished by the rotatory musculature of the upper arm. If the axis of the upper arm were fixed, however, no double lever would result. The situation would be similar to the one of turning an object with a firm fist, for which the effort is much greater.

Since the upper arm is movable around the pivot of the shoulder joint, the rotation of the upper arm alone is sufficient to make the forearm move like a seesaw: It causes one end, the elbow, to move up and down, while the other end, the hand, describes the counter motion. This fact is very important; it seems to contradict what we see. The rather large movement of the *entire* arm connected with the double lever movement of the forearm uses only a small part of the energy that would be necessary to move only the forearm. We can easily see that this up-and-down movement of the elbow is passive and does not use the muscles that normally execute this movement. Move the right upper arm up and down quickly, the forearm, held at an angle, moving along with it. By placing the left hand in the armpit one can feel the muscles working hard with each downward movement.

Now move the upper arm up and down in the same way, but let a pivot point be formed in the middle of the forearm (the wrist must not be moved, however). Even with a very active movement no muscles can be felt protruding. Except for the muscles necessary for holding up the arm, only the rotatory muscles of the upper arm are active. For a beginner this double lever movement is sometimes difficult since it uses muscles not usually involved in such a movement. As an aid to learning the proper coordination remember the movement of shaking a box of matches to find out its contents.

To return to the cello: In the third kind of string change the double lever is used. The elbow moves from its old position past its new position. At the moment of the change the seesaw process described above takes place. The hand moves—quite quickly—to its new position while the elbow moves in the opposite direction. The energy expenditure is minimal, any shaking is neutralized within the arm, and the rhythmical impulse of the double lever movement coincides with the moment of the audible change.

From the tip to somewhat below the middle of the bow we can use the double lever for any string change. It is important that the forearm and hand form a unit; the wrist should not move actively in addition. A small elastic passive movement of the wrist may be discerned, however.

In all three possibilities the angle of the hand adjusts to that of the bow by itself. The pronation position in relation to the bow is the same on the new string as on the previous one. (If the upper arm and forearm are held horizontally, with the forearm at an angle, the palm will open toward the ground. If the upper arm is held in toward the body without making an active pronation movement, the palm will open to the left.)

An oft-discussed alternative lets the wrist take care of the entire string change. It has several disadvantages as compared to the method discussed above:

1. The hand must flex excessively in both directions at the tip to take care of the great distances.

2. The pronation pressure will be less in the upper (dorsal) position than in the lower (volar) position (see Fig. 66).

3. Since the hand is pronated at the tip, a movement per-

pendicular to the palm would create an unwanted bow stroke instead of an inaudible string change. It would require an uncomfortable combination of vertical *and* lateral movements (volar-adduction movements and dorsal-abduction movements, respectively) in order to have the same length of bow on both strings in a legato string change. In fact, in a continuous change between two strings one can often hear that the down bow is loud or long on the upper string and soft or short on the lower one; in the up bow the reverse is true.

4. The arm must be pulled along sooner or later if it is not to stay on the track corresponding to the first string. Thus a complicated mechanism of subsequent adjusting movements must be used.

5. The hand must be moved up and down as a whole; there is no opposing weight involved, as with the double lever. It is therefore an error to believe that a pure wrist movement would require less energy than the double lever movement of the forearm. The jolt created by the string change using the wrist is so great that it endangers the contact with the string at the tip; the double lever, in contrast, does not produce a jolt.

We see now that the double lever movement fulfils the demands of the instrument during the string change in the upper part of the bow in an ideal way. Near the middle of the bow the range of movement becomes smaller, and the closer the change is to the frog the smaller the distance between the strings for the hand. The advantage we have at the tip, where the necessary change of angle is provided by the upper arm movement, gradually disappears. The change of angle must be actively taken over by forearm rotation.

In a passage of continuous string changes, such as that shown in Fig. 71, how can the double lever movement (which is a rota-

FIGURE 71

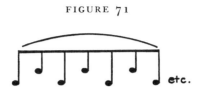

tion of the upper arm) be connected with the forearm rotation and vice versa? To examine this process closely we must deal with the circumstances of string change at the frog. Since the processes are very complicated the reader is asked to perform the following movements on his or her own instrument.

Put the bow on the G string at the frog. The hand will be slightly abducted in the wrist, that is, flexed to the right and down (Fig. 72). Now make *only* a pronation movement, without changing the forearm axis. The bow changes its angle to the string, but it leaves the string in the process. This result can be avoided in the following ways:

FIGURE 72

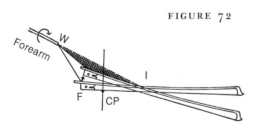

W: Wrist,
F: Frog,
I: Intersection of the extended forearm axis with the bow,
CP: Contact point of bow and string
The triangle WFI rotates around the WI axis in front of the plane of the drawing.

1. In addition to the pronation movement the wrist should move toward the middle of the body; in supination, that is, during the change from an upper to a lower string, it should move away from the body in a corresponding way.

2. No pronation should be used for the first few centimeters of the bow; in this area the string change should be achieved using only the fingers. The alternate flexion of the index finger and the little finger will make a change of angle possible.

Both movements are possible and applicable. In most cases one can avoid making the change in the last few centimeters of the bow, but if that is not possible, the author would suggest execution with the fingers, but this should not be a hard and fast rule. At a distance of 5–7 centimeters (2–3 inches) from the frog, using only finger movement will block the string change, i.e., the pressure will increase and diminish unless the process is complemented by forearm rotation.

Now put the bow down on the G string about 15 centimeters (6 inches) from the frog (Fig. 73). Using only a pronation movement with no compensation you will get an almost perfect string change. The hand and frog rotate around the axis of the forearm, whose imaginary extension goes through the contact point of the bow and the string. Only at this point of the bow does rotation of the forearm *alone* produce a string change. A little closer to the tip the pronation movement does not produce any movement, but only increases the pressure on the lower string.

In order to show the need for a compensating movement let us consider the change from a higher to a lower string. Put the bow on the D string about 25 centimeters (10 inches) from the frog. Try to use *only* forearm rotation, in this case, supination. At this distance from the frog, the bow will leave the string if you do not change the angle formed by the forearm and the hand

FIGURE 73

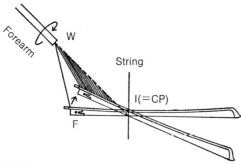

W: Wrist,
F: Frog,
I: Intersection of the extended forearm axis with the bow,
CP: Contact point of bow and string
The triangle WFI rotates around the WI axis in front of the plane of the drawing.
I coincides with CP.

(Fig. 74). With the help of supination, lift the bow *above* the G string. Now put it on the string by means of a small volar wrist movement. As the distance between intersection point *I* and contact point *C* increases in the course of a down bow, the wrist movement that keeps the bow from being lifted off the string must become bigger until it is replaced by the double lever movement of the arm at a point below the middle of the bow.

The question now arises: Why not dispense with the wrist movement completely as a compensation for the "height" since we have the double lever movement of the arm at our disposal? In the experiment with the match box we saw that the movement of the hand during the double lever mechanism is always perpendicular to the plane defined by the upper arm and forearm. If the

FIGURE 74

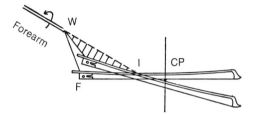

W: Wrist,
F: Frog,
I: Intersection of the extended forearm axis with the bow,
CP: Contact point of bow and string
The triangle WFI rotates around the WI axis behind the plane of the drawing;
the bow leaves the string.

upper arm is kept in a horizontal position the movement will be perpendicular to the ground; if the upper arm is allowed to hang close to the body, the movement of the hand will be horizontal and the palm will open to the left.

Of course, we cannot play with a horizontal upper arm in the lower part of the bow. With hanging elbow, however, the movement of the hand is parallel to the bow when we use the double lever; in this position the double lever movement instead of changing strings, produces a bow stroke. Another obstacle is of a physiological nature: The double lever movement can hardly be combined with the active pronation or supination movement necessary at this point. It can, however, be combined with a slight wrist movement; the latter in turn can easily be combined with a forearm rotation. Instead of trying to merge the double lever and the forearm rotation into one movement, we can use the small wrist movement to connect the two; this connection is most advantageous at the instrument and also physiologically appropriate. After a short phase in which only the wrist moves, the hand, by its bouncing up and down slightly, helps the double lever mechanism to get started.

Approaching this process from the direction of the tip, we have first of all a small wrist motion along with the double lever. To the extent to which the double lever movement is reduced, the wrist motion takes over and is combined with forearm rotation in the further course of the bow. At the moment that the extension of the forearm axis coincides with the contact point of the bow and the string, pure forearm rotation remains, which is replaced by pure finger movement in the last inches before the frog.

That is how a smooth transition from forearm rotation to whole-arm movement looks in detail. It is not absolutely necessary that the player know all these details; most cellists get similar results by imitation and trial and error. But if we attempt to describe these processes, we must do so thoroughly and in some detail; expressions like "inaudible transition" and "merging" are not really descriptive. They only set the goals we are all attempting to reach.

Let us summarize:

1. Right at the frog pure forearm rotation is not possible; we can change strings here by combining forearm rotation with a forearm movement (away from and toward the body) or, better still, by flexing and extending the fingers to varying degrees.

2. In the lower part of the bow, at a distance of about 7 centimeters (3 inches) from the frog, it is chiefly the forearm rotation that bridges the angle between the two bow tracks.

3. The closer to the middle we get in the down bow, the more this rotation is combined with a wrist motion perpendicular to the palm (dorsal and volar movement).

4. Since double lever movement and forearm rotation cannot be combined easily, but since both can be combined with a wrist

motion, such a motion is used near the balance point of the bow as a connection.

5. The closer we get to the tip, the greater the distance between bow tracks becomes for the hand. In order to bridge this distance we use the double lever movement from a point below the middle of the bow to the tip.

There is one final thing to watch in a string change. Fig. 66 shows that in the transition from a high to a low bow track, the rigid index finger increases the pronation pressure when the hand moves to the lower track without adjusting the resulting change of angle by supination. We can play the figure in Fig. 75 with prac-

FIGURE 75

tically no visible pronation movement because the double stop requires twice as much pressure as the first tone does. With a rigid index finger the change of angle alone provides the additional pressure.

FIGURE 76

In the reverse case, Fig. 76, we need not only a pronation *movement* to compensate for the change in angle (at least in the lower third of the bow) but also pronation *pressure* for the increase necessary for the double stop. This mechanism is shown in Fig. 77.

FIGURE 77

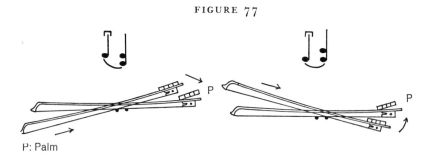

P: Palm

A delicate handling of the pronation movement is required for the artistic rendering of the music we play. The above observations, however, show that even on a purely technical plane, subtle adjustments are necessary to meet the demands of the varying physical conditions.

Simultaneous Bow and String Change

We can deduce the movements for a simultaneous bow and string change from our observations in connection with the string change. Since the bow must approach the new string during the stroke on the previous one, there is a difference in whether the passage in Fig. 78 is started with an up bow or with a down bow.

FIGURE 78

As we saw in Fig. 65, a wrist motion perpendicular to the palm (volar) with the forearm pronated results in a small bow movement on the string in the direction of the down bow, i.e., it produces a short tone.*

A pure dorsal-volar movement on two strings will produce Fig. 79. According to Fig. 65, half of the volar movement in a down

FIGURE 79

bow affects the upper string, the other half the lower string (Fig. 80). In the up bow it is the other way around.

FIGURE 80

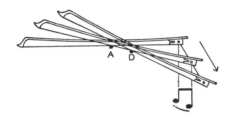

If the second and the fourth tones of Fig. 79 are omitted, resulting in Fig. 81, the pure dorsal-volar movement must be changed so that the second half no longer produces a sound. That

---

* This wrist movement is not eliminated completely by the double lever movement; it results from a passive bouncing movement of the hand. In fast string changes this bouncing movement can become an active wrist motion. Below the middle of the bow, where the double lever can no longer be used and where forearm rotation cannot yet be used, we also rely on an active dorsal-volar movement of the wrist.

FIGURE 81

can be done by reaching for the new bow track with a vertical movement. The entire movement forms a rhombus (Fig. 82). In practical application it changes into an ellipse that coincides with the comfortable movement of the hand perpendicular to the palm.

FIGURE 82

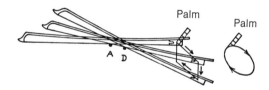

In the reverse order, Fig. 83, the effective stroke, during which the bow must approach the new string, must be accomplished by

FIGURE 83

the *lateral* wrist movement, by abduction and adduction (Fig. 84). The pure volar-dorsal movement, which is ideal for the hand, does not occur at all.

FIGURE 84

It is recommended, therefore, at least for the upper part of the bow, that one let the movement be executed as far as possible by the double lever function of the whole arm. If the elbow is held relatively low the double lever mechanism will have the desired lateral direction. (If the upper arm hangs down vertically it will move in the direction of the stroke.)

In the lower part of the bow, the hand is pronated less. To the extent to which the double lever movement is reduced, the wrist can participate in the string change by a dorsal-volar movement while the stroke is being produced by the arm movement only, as in Fig. 85. The uncomfortable abduction and adduction

FIGURE 85

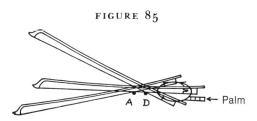

movement of the wrist is avoided, but we are forced to coordinate two movements running in different directions: the horizontal bowing movement of the arm and the vertical string change of the wrist, which is replaced by forearm rotation near the frog.

Fig. 86 represents the easier string change plus bow change, in which both changes are more or less combined in one movement, the comfortable dorsal-volar flexion, which can be used all the way from the tip to close to the frog.

FIGURE 86

XI

DIFFERENT KINDS
OF BOWING

Détaché

IN PRINCIPLE, the *détaché* stroke is part of the whole-bow stroke. At medium speed the détaché movement of the arm corresponds to the appropriate phase of Fig. 49, which shows the course of the entire stroke. A fast détaché, however, deviates from this scheme.

During a whole-bow stroke in the lower half of the bow, it is the upper arm, or better still the whole arm, that takes care of the movement. For a fast movement in the lower half of the bow, the whole arm would therefore have to be accelerated and decelerated for each individual fast stroke. The energy and movement necessary would be considerable and uneconomical for short, fast strokes. The muscle activity of the whole arm would reverberate through the entire body, and each stroke would disturb the equilibrium. To counteract these jolts, the muscles of the trunk would have to be activated; that would require considerable effort and would make the body tight.

However, there is a way of reducing this effort. For the stroke in the lower half of the bow the upper arm hangs down. If we use the mechanism of upper arm rotation instead of moving the upper arm back and forth from the body, the forearm and hand will describe an arc of a circle (with the elbow as the pivot point). This arc corresponds to the bow track needed for short strokes, i.e., to the same track that will result from a lateral movement of the upper arm. In this way only the weight of the forearm must be accelerated and decelerated for fast back-and-forth movements.

The forearm, in turn, tosses the wrist back and forth and thus augments the movement of the bow. It is advisable to hold the forearm in a rather pronated position in order to profit from the range of the wrist movement, which is wider in the dorsal-volar direction than in the horizontal direction of adduction and abduction. In this way we can achieve a rather broad back-and-forth movement of the bow without jolting the body and produce a broad détaché at a fast tempo. On the C string the situation for this kind of détaché is much less favorable than on the A string; as is shown in Fig. 49, on the C string the upper-arm movement has a larger component in the lateral direction.

For a détaché in the middle of the bow, the component of the flexion and extension in the elbow increases, and the rotation of the upper arm is gradually reduced. It is recommended that the elbow not be held too high so that the energy-saving rotation of the upper arm can be used as long as possible.

In the upper part of the bow and at the tip, the flexion and extension of the elbow remains as the sole active movement. From Fig. 49 we see that the upper arm moves down when approaching the tip in a down bow. This movement of the upper arm against the forearm (upper arm moves to the left when the forearm moves to the right) is clearly visible in a détaché at the tip, even though it is generated (passively) from activating the flexing and extending muscles of the forearm. This movement is a variation of the double lever. Again a pivot point is formed in the middle of the forearm; in this case it moves along somewhat in the direction of the hand (see Fig. 87). If we wished to prevent the passive movement of the upper arm considerable effort would be required.

FIGURE 87

Seen from above

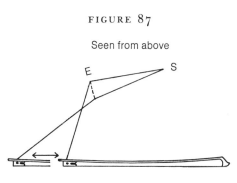

S: Shoulder, E: Elbow

Because of the speed of the back-and-forth movement, the compensating wrist movement of the bow change almost disappears in the upper half of the bow. The change is executed without a release in pressure and with great acceleration at the beginning of each tone. This is an attack with prefixed pressure, producing a tone of plosive character, just as the term *détaché* implies. Strictly speaking, even in this case each tone ends with a deceleration and starts with an acceleration, but such a short phase is of no consequence considering the speed of the entire movement.

Martellato

The *martellato* is a stroke that uses a prefixed pressure for each attack. While in the détaché the bow changes without a break and without a decrease in pressure, the martellato demands a short break before each attack, during which the pressure is prefixed. After a strong plosive sound the volume is immediately reduced, so that the impression of an especially forceful "hammered" attack is created.

The mechanism that prefixes the pressure is again pronation combined with a correspondingly stiffened index finger. Let us stress once more, however, that the visible pronation movement does not indicate how much the pressure has increased. If the index finger yields, the increase in pressure is less the bigger the visible movement. It is therefore advisable to keep the index finger stiff for all staccato and martellato bowings and to produce the increase in pressure only by pronating the forearm. Even in this case a pronation *movement* is visible because of the elasticity of the hand and the softness of the flesh. But only if the index finger is prefixed, does the movement in fact indicate the increase in pressure.

The same holds true when the pressure is decreased. It is possible to reduce it without a visible supination movement by reducing the stiffening of the index finger and the pronation pressure equally. But considering the speed with which the pressure must be reduced, it is simpler to diminish the pressure of the stiff index finger with a supination movement.

One more factor must be considered with respect to the prefixing of the pressure by pronation. Imagine that the axis of the forearm is extended beyond the wrist; the bow stick and the fingers will lie below it. If the axis rotates, the hand will describe a small arc around it; pronation *alone* produces a small down-bow stroke, supination *alone* a small up-bow stroke (see Fig. 88). In order to avoid this unintentional stroke, the forearm must be moved, to some extent, in the direction of the up bow for each pronation movement (this is implied in prefixing the pressure), regardless of whether the following tone falls on a down bow or an up bow (Fig. 89).

For martellato and staccato bowings with prefixed pressure, the speed must be full by the beginning of the tone and the pres-

FIGURE 88

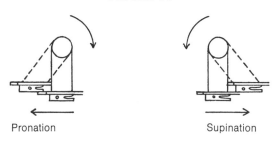

Pronation   Supination

Cross Section of the Forearm

FIGURE 89

sure must be reduced a little after the attack. If we begin the tone itself with a supination movement (that is, in the up bow) after the pressure is fixed by pronation, the conditions are ideal:

1. The movement of the bow resulting from supination is added to the speed of the arm (Fig. 65).
2. Supination reduces the pressure.

Since the supination movement in the up bow makes additional speed available for the bow and since this increase is subtracted again during the pronation (i.e., when the pressure is fixed for the next tone), the forearm, by rotating periodically, produces an almost even stroke movement when several short notes are played on one up bow.

When several short notes are played on one down bow, however, there will be a disruption of the movement of the forearm
because the forearm makes a small up-bow movement during each
successive fixation. Thus in a down bow, the forearm must travel
farther than the bow for each single stroke (Fig. 90). That is why

FIGURE 90

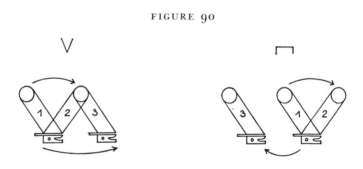

several short notes on one bow are much easier to realize on an
up bow than on a down bow. For short down bows near the frog
this disadvantage is partly reduced because no pronation is needed
to prefix the pressure; it is applied to the string from above.

It is a characteristic of the martellato sound that the tone becomes weaker after a strong attack. It was mentioned before that,
as a modification from the basic scheme of sound production, we
may keep a sound vibrating in a diminuendo with very little pressure. The bow and the string are no longer in static friction, but
the impulse of the sliding friction creates an extension of the
vibrations, so that we can speak of an "artificial reverberation."
The sound becomes bell-like, as if the bow had left the string and
let the string vibrate freely. Indeed, this latter possibility exists
between the balance point and the frog: The bow leaves the string
and then quickly fixes the pressure again for the following martellato stroke.

This martellato should not be confused with an off-the-string bowing that has a similar sound effect and for which the lower part of the bow is thrown on the string and the stroke is created by the same impulse. The pressure and the speed increase together, thus guaranteeing that the string speaks. In the martellato, however, the starting speed must be abrupt, must correspond to the prefixed pressure, and may not be increased later. If the string does not speak, it is often because the difference between the two types of bowing was not clearly observed.

Staccato

The *staccato* is no different in sound from a short martellato. Up to a certain speed nothing changes in principle from the execution of the martellato. The forearm rotation again provides the mechanism for fixing the pressure.

A fast staccato, played back and forth, turns into a détaché at a certain tempo (which differs from person to person), since, in a fast tempo, the even alternation between pronation and supination, which is necessary for the fixation of the pressure and for the subsequent tone, can no longer be executed.

The virtuoso staccato on one bow is more difficult. It is not possible to recommend any one way to execute it because different players achieve it in basically different ways. Some players are able to produce quite a fast staccato by rotating the forearm quickly and rhythmically. Another way of achieving a good staccato, at least in the up bow, requires that the wrist be able to move up and down quickly in the dorsal-volar direction. For many people this shaking seems easier than an equally fast rotation of the forearm. Pronating the forearm and making a dorsal or volar movement with the hand will produce a movement at an angle to the normal bow track (Fig. 91), as was mentioned in connection with the bow change at the tip. The component that makes the bow deviate

FIGURE 91

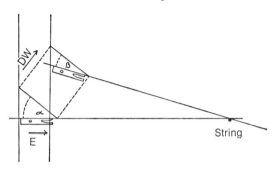

DW: Dorsal movement of the wrist,
E: Effective stroke

slightly from its track can be ignored; it is important that the dorsal movement produce a small up-bow stroke with the highest pressure at the beginning of the tone.

In practicing there are two ways in which this dorsal-volar shaking movement can be trained:

1. By consciously innervating the flexing and extending muscles of the wrist.

2. By pressing the thumb against the other fingers. When the arm is allowed to hang loosely, the thumb hangs opposite the index and middle fingers. If the fingers are pressed together abruptly, a sudden volar movement results in the wrist. (The flexion of the hand and the fingers is partly achieved by the same muscles. Their tendons pass through the wrist.)

Generally a more even shaking movement can be achieved with the second exercise.

The difficulty in this wrist staccato is that the process must take place with a constant pronation pressure, since the movement of the wrist alone, especially at the tip, transmits too little pressure to the string. The coordination of the pronation pressure and the wrist movement plus a movement of the forearm in the up bow requires exact self-observation and concentration on the disengagement of all other muscles .

For many players neither way, forearm rotation or wrist movement, brings satisfactory results, despite intensive practicing. For them there is a third possibility: Use no wrist or forearm rotatory movements, but fix the pressure on the string and make shaking movements in the elbow with a stiff arm. This method seems to run counter to all principles of movement but can nevertheless produce acoustically good results in the up bow. The tightening of the arm assures the evenness of the shaking. This evenness is supported if the upper arm (the elbow) is allowed to yield to each jerky movement in the elbow joint (so that the elbow moves back). The latter movement was discussed earlier, in connection with the détaché in the upper part of the bow (Fig. 87).

A staccato on the down bow is a different matter. If the process in Fig. 91 (for the up bow) were reversed, the pressure would be lowest at the beginning of the tone and would increase until the end. This would produce a wave effect of changing volume but not the typical staccato sound with the sharp attack at the beginning of each tone.

There is a "trick" that can be applied nowhere else in cello technique that can be used for the down-bow staccato: Lower the wrist, i.e., bring the hand into an extremely dorsal position, and execute the staccato by rotating the upper arm. Since the finger and the stick are now above the imaginary continuation of the forearm axis, the supination produces a small movement in the direction of the down bow (a normal position produces one in the direction of the up bow) (see Fig. 92). Supination always means reduced pressure. It is therefore possible to have the greatest pressure at the beginning of each down-bow movement and thus avoid the necessity of the small movements of the forearm in the opposite direction for each individual pressure fixation.

FIGURE 92

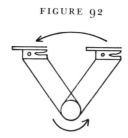

Instead of pronating and supinating the forearm we can execute a double lever movement of the forearm with the elbow as low as possible. The pivot point is at about the same point of the forearm as is used for the double lever movement of the string change. The upper arm rotation is the "motor." This double lever movement produces an even, passive rotation of the forearm, which makes it possible for the hand to play a good down-bow staccato at least in the upper part of the bow.

All this shows that the mechanism of the down bow in this kind of staccato is completely different from that of the up bow.

Off-the-String Bowings

In off-the-string bowings the elastic hair of the bow produces a rebound on the elastic string. Because of the momentarily increased tension of the hair and the string, the bow bounces off.

The elasticity of the bow is not the same at all points. If an object is allowed to fall on the tightened hair of the bow, we can see that the bow is more elastic in the middle and less so toward the tip and the frog. If the bow is allowed to drop on the string, the hand will partly absorb the effect of the rebounding bow, the more so the closer to the frog the bow bounces. From these two facts we may conclude that the most effective elasticity of the bow is a little above the middle, where the elasticity of the bow has not yet decreased very much and where the absorbing effect of the hand is reduced.

If the bow is allowed to fall on the string without any activity of the hand, the height of the rebound decreases with each successive bounce. At the same time, the interval between the individual tones becomes shorter and shorter until the original falling energy has been consumed.

In all off-the-string bowings this natural process must be regulated so that exact dynamic and rhythmic control of single tones is possible. There are several possibilities:

1. In playing a series of off-the-string notes on one bow, we can make use of the fact that the effective elasticity of the bow increases between the middle and the upper third of the bow. The index finger can provide pressure to decrease the natural rebound height. The next tone then follows after a shorter time. The pressure of the index finger makes the next tone stronger than the short distance from the string would suggest, but still a little weaker than the previous tone, since no new source of energy compensates for the loss. In a series of notes on one down bow, the height of the bounce and therefore the time between the notes can be kept constant by gradually decreasing the pressure of the index finger. However, each successive tone will be weaker until the original bouncing energy has been used up. With some practice we can achieve a series of about sixteen short notes, each decreasing in volume. In practical playing this kind of figure is rare, but there is occasionally a passage of four notes that we can manage satisfactorily in this way.

In the up bow the circumstances are less favorable. The absorbing effect of the hand increases with each tone so that only a small number of tones can be controlled rhythmically, and after a short time the rebounding ceases.

2. In a relatively slow series of off-the-string notes—on one bow or back and forth—it seems reasonable to produce each tone with a small pronation movement that will compensate each time for the lost bouncing energy. The volume and the rhythm are controlled by the index finger. A big disadvantage of this kind of execution is that the amount of pressure for each tone must be extremely accurate to maintain the rhythm, which in this case depends directly on the pressure of the index finger. This kind of bowing has its physical limits at a certain speed, since each tone must be executed by a double movement of the right arm (pronation and supination). It therefore cannot be used for a virtuoso spiccato.

3. For the third method we must first examine the movement of the part of the bow that touches the string during the *spiccato*. The bow falls on the string at an angle. The first phase of the tone is slightly choked, i.e., the tone does not have a pizzicato-like beginning but makes a typical "scratchy" noise during the first vibrations. This noise is so short, however, that it is not perceived as such but as a plosive attack, characteristic of the spiccato. A short phase follows in which the string vibrates at its full amplitude. In the last phase the string vibrates freely after the bow has left the string (see Fig. 93). If the angle at which the bow reaches the string is too steep the first phase produces a noise; if it is too flat the string does not speak and the bow is tossed back before the string reaches its full amplitude.

By moving the frog in a direction parallel to the bouncing part of the bow, that is, approximately in a semi-circle, we can influence the rhythmic process of the rebound. Put the instrument down flat. Hold the bow with just two fingers and move the frog parallel to the contact point of the bow. The bow will not change its angle during the movement. Depending on the height of the

FIGURE 93

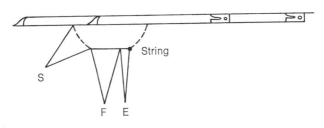

S: Starting phase of the vibration,

F: Full amplitude,

E: Ending phase of the vibration

movement, we can achieve an evenly recurring rebound that requires no further source of energy.

The reason is that the entire weight of the bow is available for the *bounce;* the *rebound,* however, is supported by the active lifting of the frog so that only part of the entire weight must be bounced back. Thus more energy is available for the bounce than the rebound consumes. We must therefore look for movements of the arm that can achieve a parallel movement, namely, a semicircle.

First, the wrist comes to mind. By combining the dorsal-volar movement with a back-and-forth stroke of the forearm or of the hand (abduction and adduction), we can produce a good spiccato which is rhythmically and dynamically controlled (Fig. 94). The

FIGURE 94

stiff index finger need not move itself; before the bow has finished its natural rebound it "hits" the fixed index finger. As a consequence, no visible forearm rotation results.

In addition to determining the height of the fall, the wrist (or better still, the index finger) is able to give a strong or weak impulse; the rhythm is not disturbed by this impulse since it, too, is determined by the wrist. The fact that the force of the impulse as well as the height of the fall are determined by the wrist makes us highly independent rhythmically and dynamically from the elasticity of the point on the bow being used. Since, starting from the frog, the rebound effect increases toward and beyond the middle of the bow, the tones become increasingly shorter the further the contact point is from the frog. Thus, this kind of spiccato can be played piano or forte at the same point of the bow and in the same rhythm. It is therefore not quite right to insist that a loud spiccato *must* be played close to the frog.

When we examined the transmission of pressure we found a point for each volume at which no rotational force was active and at which the change from pronation to supination occurred. It seems obvious that we should use this fact for the dynamic determination of the spiccato. A stroke without rotational force will result in more pressure at the frog than at a point closer to the tip. That fact deserves some consideration, but it should be remembered that the elasticity of the bow decreases toward the frog and we soon reach a limit at which no rebound is possible. The bow must then be actively lifted off the string.

As the tempo is increased, even the third kind of spiccato reaches its limit, a speed at which the necessary double movement per individual stroke (a dorsal *and* a volar movement for each tone) can no longer be realized. We must therefore look for movements that require only one movement per stroke.

4. The index finger may provide such a movement. If it is

alternately flexed and extended on the bow stick for each single movement, the fingertip will describe an arc around the axis of the middle joint of the index finger (see Fig. 95). This movement

FIGURE 95

is not big, but for a fast spiccato it matches the arc that the contact point of the bow describes.

The rhythm is totally dependent on the movement of the index finger, which determines the volume by the strength of the impulse. In order to expand the length of the stroke, the adduction and abduction of the wrist may be coordinated with the movement of the index finger. That is not difficult even in a fast tempo, since each stroke requires only one movement in one direction.

It is essential for this kind of spiccato that the index finger be able not only to exert pressure but also to lift up the bow actively, away from the string, with the help of the static friction between the bow and the finger. (See the discussion of the pressure relationships within the hand in chap. 9.)

The spiccato requires a movement of the index finger similar to that of the pizzicato: alternate flexion and extension. The additional abduction and adduction fits this analogy, too, because the pizzicato also requires a coordinated wrist movement, in this case, mainly in the dorsal-volar direction. Therefore we can say that in a fast spiccato, the index finger "plucks" the bow stick.

In an abducted hand position, the index finger must be flexed in any case if the angle formed by bow and the string and therefore the contact point are not to change. An abduction and adduction movement of the bow hand thus almost naturally provides the flexion and extension of the index finger that produces the spiccato. In this way we can increase the speed of the spiccato to a point sufficient for most virtuoso passages.

5. For extremely fast tone repetitions there is another kind of movement, the *sautillé*. Normally the bow is moved on a track that corresponds to its extension in both directions. If the bow is brought into a position that forms an acute angle with its track, a bounce can be achieved that receives its energy directly from the bow movement. Even though the angle may be small, it will contain a small movement component perpendicular to the bow, which will produce a corresponding rebound (see Fig. 96). For the hand this movement is circular, or better still, elliptical. If

FIGURE 96

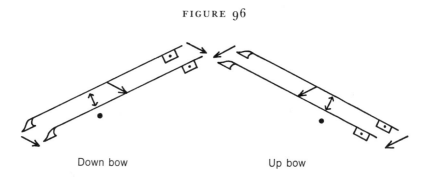

Down bow   Up bow

the forearm is shaken back and forth on a slightly diagonal track, the loosely hanging hand describes an ellipse without any additional muscle action (see Fig. 97).

FIGURE 97

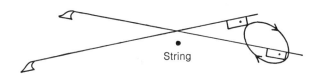

String

A rebound of the bow stick also results if the hair has not yet left the string at the beginning of such a shaking movement. In this case if the bow stick is pressed on the hair that touches the string, the tension will increase and result in a rebound. After several repetitions this movement becomes a true spiccato, in which the hair leaves the string. That is why it is often said that the spiccato comes "automatically" at a certain place on the bow and at the right speed of tone repetition. However, a back-and-forth movement *within* the bow track will never result in a spiccato, no matter what the speed or what the point of the bow. A component perpendicular to the plane of the bow and the string must be involved in any case.

In this extremely fast kind of spiccato the rhythm is determined by the shaking of the forearm; the extent of the rebound has no influence on the rhythm since the hand forces the bow back to the string. However, a spiccato can only be achieved in this way if we stay in the most elastic part of the bow.

6. The fact that the elasticity of the bow diminishes toward the frog suggests another off-the-string bowing for our repertoire. Between the balance point and the frog no rebound is possible. While in 3. and 4. the bow was lifted up actively (with the wrist or, better still, with the finger) and the remaining weight was left to the rebound, in an off-the-string bowing at the frog the entire weight of the bow would have to be lifted up to *simulate* a re-

bound. For a rebound without rotational force the pressure on the string increases as we approach the frog, since below the balance point the hand must exercise additional vertical pressure to counterbalance the weight of the bow.

That is necessary only for the bounce without any rotational force; it does not mean that we cannot play soft tones with a rebound effect at the balance point and closer to the frog. If the rotational force is slightly negative, that is, in a supinated position, correspondingly less pressure reaches the string during the semicircular movement.

Since no rebound occurs below the balance point, the length of the tone can be determined freely. After the attack from the air, the tone is treated just like a détaché stroke. The speed of such a series of tones, however, is limited since the whole arm must be moved along. In somewhat faster passages the movement of the arm corresponds to that of the détaché in the lower part of the bow.

The attack of a tone is softer in an off-the-string bowing at the balance point than in a martellato at the same point with prefixed pressure. While the martellato has a sharp plosive beginning, the off-the-string bowing at the balance point consists of an increase in pressure combined with an increase in speed, even if the hand moves absolutely evenly. The speed of the bow is reduced at the moment of the attack because of the frictional resistance of the string, and is immediately increased again by the continuous arm movement. The hand yields a little to this process, as we can observe.

In an off-the-string bowing at the balance point we therefore should avoid additional active hand or forearm movements since at this point there is no rotational force that might justify a pronation movement; otherwise an additional supination in the up bow (as is necessary for the martellato) would result in too much speed at the moment of the attack and the string therefore would not speak properly.

Let us summarize:

1. The bouncing bow has the tendency to make each tone softer than the previous one and closer to it in time.
2. There are different ways of influencing this process so that rhythmic and dynamic control, that is, evenness, are possible:

    a. By reducing the pressure gradually (for fast tones on one bow). Rhythmic evenness will result. This means is rarely used, however.
    b. By pronating in regular cycles. The energy loss for each tone will be compensated for. This means can hardly be recommended because the energy cannot be controlled easily and because the speed is limited.
    c. By moving the frog parallel to the bouncing part of the bow. The wrist will describe an arc of a circle. For a moderately fast spicatto this way is ideal, but the speed is limited (double movement volarly *and* dorsally per individual stroke).
    d. By flexing and extending the index finger. This will again result in an arc of a circle at the frog and therefore in a parallel movement of the bow. Methods c. and d. will produce the actual, full-sounding, controlled spiccato. Of course, a combination of wrist and finger movement is possible.
    e. By letting the bow fall on the string at an angle. The hand will describe an ellipse. This method is advisable only at a very fast tempo; it must be used in the part of the bow that is most elastic.

f. At the balance point a movement of the entire arm is possible; since elasticity has no practical importance here any more, the length of the tone may be controlled just as in an on-the-string bowing. The bow must be lifted off the string actively.

3. An off-the-string bowing is softer than a martellato bowing.

4. The dynamics are less dependent on the height of the fall than on the force of the impulse of the wrist or the finger. Therefore there is only a limited advantage in moving closer to the frog for loud spiccato. The difference between a spiccato close to the frog and one close to the middle is more one of attack and duration than of volume.

CONCLUSION

THE PHYSICS of sound on string instruments has been sufficiently investigated for practical application. But knowledge of the physics of sound is only one of several important conditions for masterful playing. It is surprising that string pedagogy has barely tried to examine the energy and weight relationships of bodily movements, for, as we have seen, they are the exact counterpart of our physiological processes and therefore of our playing sensations. Without also considering the physical "mirror" of energy and weight relationships, a detailed examination of the physiological motor functions is not possible. These physiological processes, in turn, are closely related to the player's emotional state, expression, and playing personality.

Even detailed explanations of positions, intended to make the playing easier, do not penetrate to the center of the playing experience. This experience consists of the dynamic movement, of the way in which the movements develop. A good player will be able to play in an extremely uncomfortable position; for example, if he holds the bow in his fist, he will still play "more correctly" than someone who follows the position instructions in detail but whose curves of movement are physically wrong and consequently lead to uneasiness and technical as well as psychological insecurity.

The present attempt to analyze these movements cannot claim to be complete. Much study is still needed in order to present, in a way that can be used pedagogically, the relationship between the exterior, physical side and the inner, physiological and psychological aspects of cello playing.

Two questions must be answered in the process of learning: What must be learned? How should it be learned? The present book is limited to answering the first question. It attempts to establish the goals for the technical learning process to help the player avoid "dead-end" roads and "detours" in his practicing.

BIBLIOGRAPHY

Ansermet, Ernest. *Die Grundlagen der Musik im menschlichen Bewusstsein.* Munich: Piper, 1961.

Becker, Hugo. *Mechanik und Ästhetik des Violoncellspiels.* Vienna: Universal-Edition, 1929.

Buytendijk, F. J. J. *Allgemeine Theorie der menschlichen Haltung und Bewegung.* Berlin: Springer, 1956.

Eisenberg, Maurice. "Cello Playing of Today." *The Strad* (London), 1957.

Flesch, Carl. *Die Kunst des Violinspiels.* Berlin: Ries & Erler, 1928.

Foppa, Klaus. *Lernen, Gedächtnis, Verhalten.* Cologne and Berlin: Kiepenheuer & Witsch, 1965.

Ghiselli, Edwin, and Brown, Clarence W. *Personnel and Industrial Psychology.* 2d ed. New York: McGraw-Hill, 1955.

Grandjean, E. *Physiologische Arbeitsgestaltung.* Thun and Munich: Ott Verlag, 1963.

Groh, Herbert. *Sportmedizin.* Stuttgart: Enke-Verlag, 1962.

Heman, Christine. *Intonation auf Streichinstrumenten.* Kassel: Bärenreiter, 1964.

Hochmuth, Gerhard. *Biomechanik sportlicher Bewegungen.* Frankfurt: Wilhelm Limpert-Verlag, 1967.

Hofstetter, Peter R. *Fischer-Lexikon der Psychologie.* Frankfurt: Fischer, 1957.

Hopfer, Margarete. *Die Klanggestaltung auf Streichinstrumenten.* Leipzig: Kistner & Siegel, 1941.

Jacobs, Dore. *Die menschliche Bewegung.* Ratingen: Aloys Henn-Verlag, 1962.

Polnauer, Frederick, and Marks, Morton. *Senso-motor Study and Its Application to Violin Playing.* Urbana, Ill.: American String Teachers' Association, 1964.

Rein, H., and Schneider, M. *Physiologie des Menschen.* Berlin: Springer, 1960.

Rohracher, Hubert. *Einführung in die Psychologie.* Vienna, Munich, and Berlin: Urban & Schwarzenberg, 1971.

Schmidtke, Heinz. *Untersuchungen über die Abhängigkeit der Bewegungsgenauigkeit im Raum von der Körperstellung.* Research Report, No. 941. Cologne: Kultusministerium des Landes Nordrhein-Westfalen, 1961.

——. "Der Einfluss der Bewegungsgeschwindigkeit auf die Bewegungsgenauigkeit." *Int. Zeitschr. ang. Physiol.* 17: 252, 1958.

Schmidtke, Heinz, and Stier, Fritz. *Der Aufbau komplexer Bewegungsabläufe aus Elementarbewegungen.* Research Report, No. 822. Cologne: Kultusministerium des Landes Nordrhein Westfalen, 1960.

Steinhausen, F. A. *Die Physiologie der Bogenführung.* Leipzig: Breitkopf & Härtel, 1907.

Stutschewsky, J. *Das Violoncellspiel. Neue systematische Schule.* Mainz: Schott, 1929.

Trendelenburg, Wilhelm. *Die natürlichen Grundlagen der Kunst des Streichinstrumentspiels.* Berlin: Springer, 1925.

Wellek, Albert. "Gehörpsychologie." *Musik in Geschichte und Gegenwart (MGG)*, vol. 4, col. 1571ff. Kassel: Bärenreiter, 1955.

Winkel, Fritz. "Akustik (Violine)." *Musik in Geschichte und Gegenwart (MGG)*, vol. 13, col. 1691ff. Kassel: Bärenreiter, 1955.